Misha Defonseca returned to Brussels at the end of the war, and it was there she later met her husband, Maurice. They had a son, and emigrated to the United States. She now lives near Boston, close to a wolf sanctuary, which she visits frequently.

SURVIVING WITH WOLVES

Mishke was seven years old when the Nazis took her Jewish parents from her. All she knew was that they had gone East. So one day, the little girl set out Eastwards to find them. Alone, Mishke crossed Belgium, Germany and Poland. Close to starvation, a family of wolves befriended her. She ate and played with the wolf cubs, protected by their mother. Mishke continued walking for four years, encountering many unspeakable horrors: at one point, she is forced to kill a German soldier to save her own life. Eventually, via the Ukraine, Romania and Italy, she found her way home to Belgium.

MISHA DEFONSECA

with the collaboration of Vera Lee
and Marie-Thérèse Cuny

Translated from the French
by Sue Rose

SURVIVING
WITH
WOLVES

The most extraordinary story of
World War II

Complete and Unabridged

ULVERSCROFT
Leicester

First published in Great Britain in 2005 by
Portrait, an imprint of
Piatkus Books Limited
London

First Large Print Edition
published 2006
by arrangement with
Piatkus Books Limited
London

British Library CIP Data

Defonseca, Misha
    Surviving with wolves: the most extraordinary story of
World War II.—Large print ed.—
    Ulverscroft large print series: non-fiction
    1. Defonseca, Misha—Childhood and youth
    2. Jewish children in the Holocaust—Belgium—Biography
    3. Children of disappeared persons—Belgium—Biography
    4. Human-wolf encounters—Europe
    5. World War, *1939 – 1945* —Children—Belgium—Biography
    6. Large type books
    I. Title II. Lee, Vera III. Cuny, Marie-Thérèse
    940.5'318'092

    ISBN 1–84617–439–2

Published by
F. A. Thorpe (Publishing)
Anstey, Leicestershire

Set by Words & Graphics Ltd.
Anstey, Leicestershire
Printed and bound in Great Britain by
T. J. International Ltd., Padstow, Cornwall

This book is printed on acid-free paper

Dedication

This book is dedicated to the memory of my beloved parents, to Grandpère and to Marthe, as well as to all the animals who live in my heart, so that the faces of those I will never stop loving remain vibrant with life for ever.

Contents

Prologue
Thank You, Madame

Passers-by ignore me. They don't notice that I'm a stray wolf wandering through town. A grey wolf, male or female, nameless and ageless, adrift in a sea of human indifference. I'm afraid of crowds. Awkwardly I move away from the people I meet, my nostrils quivering with disgust. I hate human skin and its stink of death.

I was a little girl when I ran away from their world. My name was Mishke, I was Jewish and I was seven years old. They caught up with me eventually, and now they make me attend college and go to mass with a ridiculous hat perched on my unruly hair. They make me wear ugly, shapeless clothes and shoes that cramp my bent claws, which are used to the damp earth in the woods. They don't look beyond my unsightly appearance, scarred by suffering. I'm covered with cuts and scabs and my feet are

1

misshapen from my long walk through their world at war. I've seen death everywhere and I've experienced cold and hunger worse than they could ever imagine. I've lived with the wolves and become a wolf myself in body and spirit. That's why they don't understand my fierce inner strength, my uncontrollable urge to bite if I'm attacked, the hunger I never manage to satisfy, or the wild freedom I've been seeking — unsuccessfully — by any means possible since they shut me away.

On this particular day in the town I'm on the trail of my former pack. Somewhere in Brussels is a street where there's a small, dingy building with a dusty, almost empty apartment, where I used to hide under the bed. That was when I was a little girl with blonde hair and green eyes. This place looks vaguely familiar, with the gleaming rails of the number 56 tramline which runs the length of the rue Gallait and serves a run-down neighbourhood of Brussels. I notice a school. Is it the one I knew, where a woman dressed in black took my hand and led me away while I was waiting for Papa? I was sitting on three grey stone steps, but I can't see those steps. Have they gone? I don't remember that porch at all. I have to pick a road. I decide to go that way. If I walk along the tramline, I should find the street where my parents lived. But there are three streets in front of me: two are straight and climb uphill, while the third curves round at an angle.

I walk up and down all three, looking up at the buildings, searching for a clue. I quickly rule out one of the streets, because I don't remember it bending round like that, which leaves the two others. The same buildings, the same balconies, identical lines of façades. I decide on one about halfway along. I think the apartment building was in the middle of a street, but it's hard to gauge distance in my memory. I was very young and it was ten years ago. It could have been further up or much further down. I slowly walk up the street again, then back down it, without spotting any detail that might jog my memory. Time is getting on and I lied to my guardians, saying I was going to college this afternoon when there weren't any lessons. For some time I've been enjoying a modicum of freedom because I'm allowed to make the journey to and from college on my own. I'm supposed to get back exactly on time. I'm not allowed any leeway, so this is the first time I've risked going into town on my own in search of my past.

It *must* be here, in this neighbourhood, behind one of these façades, or one of those on the other street, but I can't waste any more time. The people living here after the war must have known what happened, so I stop at random, right in the middle of the street, in front of the entrance to an apartment building. If this isn't it, someone is bound to tell me to try opposite or next door or a little further down. I walked thousands of miles across war-torn Europe on my own and yet here I am, lost in a tiny neighbourhood, unable to tell one balcony from another. If I were in a wood or a forest in Germany, Poland or the Ukraine, I would know how to find the wolves' lair, the hollow tree or the stone at the bend of a stream. Here, it's not so easy, and I stand uncertainly in front of these identical closed doors.

In a strange way, I feel as if I'm seven again. I'm worried that I'll be sent packing and that someone will contemptuously slam the door in my face. I'm no longer a wolf, just an awkward, skinny teenager, her scarred finger hovering over the three bells. I seem to remember the apartment being on the first floor, so I push the middle button.

Someone appears on the balcony which I hope beyond hope was once mine. A woman calls down, 'Yes?'

'May I have a word with you, please, Madame?' I'm afraid she'll be put off by my appearance. My face isn't terribly attractive, I have short, almost close-cropped hair and my skin is coarsened by the scabs I pick constantly, sometimes until they bleed. Also, I have a clumsy way of walking, weighed down by shoes that never fit properly. I take a step back, looking up bravely, ready to run away.

But the woman replies, 'I'll be right down.'

I still find it hard to express myself when I come face to face with a human stranger, because I'm very wary and because I've become too used to talking without opening my mouth. Most of the time I just talk to myself, as I did during my long years of isolation. As a result, when the woman arrives I blurt out the sentences I've formed in my head without stopping to take a breath, to avoid making any mistakes. 'Madame, my parents were arrested here during the war. They were captured with a lot of other people in the street. I think it was in this street — I wondered whether you'd heard anything about it.'

'Yes, people were arrested in this street, but also in the other one. What were your parents called?'

'I don't know.'

'But what's your surname? Don't you know your own surname?'

'No. All I know is that Maman's name was

Gerusha, and Papa's was Reuven.'

The woman looks at me in surprise. I don't want her to ask me anything else. I hate the name I have now, which isn't mine. Anyway, who cares about surnames? Does a wolf have a surname? Or a horse, or a dog? This 'Monique Valle' I've been saddled with means nothing to me. I'm Mishke and that's that. When I don't say anything, the woman — probably trying to get rid of me — quickly continues, 'When we took this place over, all we found was a box and some photos scattered over the floor. I couldn't throw them away, it was too upsetting, so my husband put them somewhere. Wait here a moment.'

She doesn't let me in, but it's kind of her to tell me about the photos and I want to see them, so I don't run away. I wait by the front door, my heart beating a little faster. Can I possibly have come to the right place? Might I recognise Maman or Papa in these photos? I don't even know if they had any photos among their things, there were so few possessions in that apartment. No furniture apart from a bed, where all three of us slept, a table and some chairs, an armchair, a few clothes hanging on the wall, and a cupboard on the landing containing a rifle hidden behind the brooms. I'm certain I saw that rifle. And there was also my hobby horse, Jules. Jules was just a soft, threadbare head attached to the end of a broom handle, an old pre-war plaything. Astride my spirited charger, I would gallop through an imaginary world. He was my friend, and I'd recognise him from his downy, tattered ears, even from his smell, if he were somewhere in this house.

I wait, gazing up and down the street. I remember there was a grocer's at the junction of two streets, and a horse that regularly clattered past our house, harnessed to a cart. It would draw to a halt just by the store and the driver would shout, 'Whoa, Jules!' to make the horse stop and 'Giddy up, Jules!' to make it move off again. That's why I called my horse Jules.

There's no grocer's at the corner of these streets, but I'm sure I'm in the right area. I once overheard someone saying that the grocer couldn't be trusted because he must have denounced various people. The grocery store may have disappeared after the war.

'Here, I've got this. Take a look. If you find anything, you can keep it.' The woman hands me a grey cardboard box, without a lid, containing stacks of photos, large and small.

I rummage around in this jumble, feeling embarrassed and awkward on the doorstep. She's waiting patiently, but I can sense she's in a hurry for me to leave, for me to say, 'No, I'm sorry, these aren't my parents,' or to choose a photo and thank her. But there are too many, and she stands there watching me as I pick up the bundle of photos and clumsily sort through them.

I've no idea how I'm supposed to react at the sight of these faces and figures on black or yellowing paper. There are numerous children as well as adults posing in various outfits and group photos. Some of them must date from before the First World War. I'm drawn to two of the largest photos: a portrait of a man, simply because he has blond hair and light eyes like my father and could be his brother; and one of a woman, who doesn't look anything like my mother. She's pretty, but not as pretty as Maman. Her smile reveals white teeth, her big eyes are a little sad, but her hair is short, unlike Maman's, which was magnificent, black and wavy. Maman was very beautiful. These aren't my parents, but I'll take these two photos, because they are of a blond man and a woman with dark hair. They're not mine, but I choose them, just as you might draw ghosts out of the shadows into the light; I choose them firstly because this woman is waiting for me to decide and also because of their symbolic value. I don't even want to know who they are and anyway there's nothing written on the back. These are forgotten parents, driven out of their home, as mine were, and who must have met with the same fate. They'll be a visible keepsake.

I shall hide them so that no one will ask me to explain, or take them away from me, or treat me like a thief or, even worse, sneer at my stubborn assertions that I'm Jewish and my name is Mishke. One day, when I'm free, I'll frame them and hang them on the wall. I'll look at them every day, as if they alone represent my unknown family. I'll make offerings of flowers and I'll light candles, as Maman did in the evening on Jewish holidays.

'I'll take these, Madame.'

'Fine.' She doesn't even ask any questions and I don't give any reasons. Deep down, she couldn't care less, despite her politeness on the doorstep. She doesn't care who these people were or who I am. I'm a nuisance. The war is over.

'I would still like to know what happened, Madame.'

'Well, we weren't here then, so we don't know anything. People round here say there were arrests and that certain people were turned out of their homes, but you'd need to try a little further up and also on the other side of the neighbourhood, because there were several round-ups in many of those streets.'

The way she's gazing at me makes me uncomfortable. It isn't at all threatening, but I need to escape. Anyway, I have to make my way back quickly. It's just late enough to guarantee me a scolding when I return and I feel so sad and disappointed by this fruitless attempt that I don't feel up to going any further. Anyway, where would I go? Ring all the bells on all the doors in the neighbourhood? Count all the three-storey apartment buildings with a first-floor balcony? Beg someone to help me remember, like some poor wretch starved of memories?

I hardly ever begged for food when I was all alone in the world, preferring to steal it. I've never begged for affection, either. Only the wolves fed me as one of their own. Although I didn't know it, I was a young wolf whom they recognised and nurtured with their prey and their warmth. They were the only ones who protected me, and it's been a mistake to try and track down my childhood memories among the humans. I won't retrace my early steps. Better to let them fade for ever. I don't care if I have no surname and I don't give a damn if I have no family.

I survived with the wolves. That experience

has marked me for life. I'm now learning to live with humans and I'm a fast learner. You don't have to like them — you just have to feel enough hatred to hold your head up high without crying. I know how to act like a human. I know all their expressions. I'm learning how to talk, read, write and wear a mask as they do. And a feeling of intense elation still sweeps over me when I think of the extraordinary experiences I've had and which they'll never share. Falling asleep in a lair, snuggling up to a she-wolf, gnawing the same bones, lying flat on the ground before the leader of the pack.

That's why the shoemaker wasn't able to do anything for my callused feet or my toes curled over like claws. My little-girl feet grew bigger in the woods, attired in anything I could find to protect them — a battered shoe, a soldier's boot, a rag, a clog. The skin became thick and hard. I would scrape it off with a knife, removing any uncomfortable calluses with my teeth and biting my toenails. When I was starving, I chewed fragments of hard skin or nail to make me feel as if I were eating. My feet caused me a great deal of pain, and still do.

You haven't the slightest idea, Madame, who 'wasn't here when they rounded up the Jews', how I waged my own war. I will honour these two portraits, which I've taken from under your nose, because these people suffered the same fate as my mother and father. And they will be far more highly honoured beneath my orphan's mattress than at the bottom of a box somewhere in a corner of your house. 'Goodbye, Madame. Thank you, Madame.'

I head back to the two women who provide my board and lodging and who are responsible for my education. Sybil and Léontine, old maids wedded to their god. They'll honk like geese because I lied and went missing. They'll call me a dawdler along with all the other names they've given me. I'm a savage, a nobody who pees in the garden instead of using the toilet like a good, grateful orphan girl. A little monster who refuses to wear ridiculous hats. A wicked girl who hates wearing cotton panties or flannelette nightdresses buttoned up to the chin. A rebel who rejects the god they've forced on me who isn't mine.

If only they knew what I hide under my mattress! The last knife I found in the woods, the compass that guided me all those years towards the rising sun, the Russian stars ripped from a dead soldier's hat. The last remaining treasures of a life spent roaming with the wolves. I change my hiding places regularly. I'm much cleverer than they think. I climb out of the windows, clamber up on to the roof, devour all the food they give me as if I'm about to run off again with the prospect of an empty stomach for days on end. They know nothing about my life, because they didn't want to know.

'No, you're not Jewish. No, your name isn't Mishke. Not another word, Monique! You must learn your prayers and recite the Hail Mary. Go and make your confession, then kneel down in the church. You are fourteen years old and you must behave like a young woman. Your name and date of birth are registered at the Town Hall. You were born on 12 May 1937, your name is Monique Valle and there's an end to the matter.'

'No, Maman told me I was born in 1934. I'm not fourteen, I'm seventeen.'

'All that's over and done with, Monique. You have a name. That will do.'

They can keep their name. I was six years old when they took away my parents, their love and my name. I was seven years old when I had to run away. I cling to this certainty and a few months won't make any difference. My identity is in my long sturdy legs, accustomed to walking and running, in my ravenous wolf's stomach and my strong white teeth which have gnawed all manner of things. I'm a strong, brave creature. I learned how to defend myself, how to attack and how to survive, all on my own. I have nothing in common with this Monique Valle, who's being sent to the local college to learn how to be a good nun or teacher.

These bigots have given me four walls and a roof, and they feed me. I shall make the most of it until they no longer have the right to shut me away. Perhaps I am a bad girl by their criteria but, even though they say they only want to help, I know perfectly well what they're trying to stifle within me. As always, I mustn't be Jewish, I must forget Mishke and the wolves and everything else. But that's something I will never do.

1

A Woman in Black

My memory of the building I was trying to find in a Brussels street is both hazy and very exact. The clearest picture I have is of going into the apartment for the first time. Maman held my hand and I can see both of us standing in a room after walking upstairs. There was a large window streaming with light, as well as the horse I named Jules. The moment I saw him, I know that I let go of my mother's hand, ran over to him and hugged and kissed him. That horse was an old plaything which had probably been left behind but, as I had nothing, he was wonderful.

The apartment smelled of dust and the room was virtually empty — I don't really remember what was in it, except for the bed and a table. Sometimes I'm afraid to try and force the memories to resurface in case I create events or objects that never really existed. I can see myself under the bed in the apartment. I sometimes hid there to play, sometimes to take refuge. A feeling of dread used to come over me occasionally, probably in the same way as an animal is affected by its master's nervousness, because Maman must have been afraid. I used to bite my nails so badly that my fingertips got sore.

I can still see a ray of sunlight coming through that window, carrying tiny dust motes. I was hungry, and I wanted to eat that shaft of light. I emerged from my hiding place, opened my mouth and swallowed what I imagined were tiny creatures in the light.

We lived in a poor neighbourhood. All I remember are a few fleeting images, more like feelings, which are fast disappearing. I often wonder why I don't remember what I knew or experienced before that apartment. All I remember clearly is that bright room and the rectangular window with a balcony. The sunshine poured in, and yet it was a narrow street and I could see the other grey houses very close up. This was probably why I was strictly forbidden to go out on the balcony.

When I was scolded, I would shut myself in the broom cupboard, which was very dark and cramped, and I'd cry, crouching next to the brooms. Even if I heard my name called, I wouldn't budge. In my childish way, I wanted them to worry about me and come looking for me. Then, one day, my behaviour changed; I stopped reacting by bursting into tears. If Maman said to me, 'I don't like you any more,' because I'd been up to some mischief, I'd reply, 'Fine, I'll like myself!'

I already had a rather rebellious streak. I hated being forbidden to go out on the balcony: 'How come other kids are allowed outside in the street when I can't even go on the balcony?' I ventured out there just once, one single time, despite being forbidden, and I felt guilty about it for many years, thinking that someone must have seen me and denounced us. I'd been longing to lean out over the street to watch people passing by, the sunlight, life on the outside. And I had great fun spitting on to passers-by from the balcony. I must have been six years old. Papa, who had gone out, saw me from the street and gave me a terrible telling-off. He was furious. 'You mustn't do that! You mustn't show yourself!'

I can still hear my mother's soft, low voice, very calm and melodious, with a Russian accent. She used to call me 'mon amour d'amour'. That day, she tried to explain why I wasn't allowed on the balcony. 'It's danger-ous, mon amour d'amour. You must try to understand.' I didn't understand. It just seemed totally unfair.

I have the impression that Papa was more like me; he was solidly built and square-shouldered, with a firm, decisive voice, which could sound rather curt. I can still see his wide face and shortish hair, which he wore slicked back. His broad forehead. He wasn't as much a part of my life as Maman, who stayed with me all day long. She never ventured out of the building. We were rather like prisoners in that room, and I was always getting under her feet, or daydreaming under the bed.

Papa often said to her, 'I'm so sorry you have to live somewhere like this!' Maman must have been from a wealthy family. She had slender wrists and delicate hands. This was not a woman accustomed to housework.

I admired her so much that I wanted to be just like her. I remember her beautiful jet-black hair, dark eyes and dusky complexion. I'd say now that she looked like a gypsy. She was slim, shapely and pretty, while I was a podgy little girl with fair skin and light eyes like Papa's. I despaired of ever looking like her. She loved to draw — she would draw my face; and I thought I looked so ugly, thickset and plain that I should have been a boy.

I was also a very possessive, jealous child, particularly when it came to their friend

Gilles, the only stranger I ever saw in the apartment. Gilles would come from time to time to bring food, and if he said, for example, 'You know, I think I'll keep your Maman company when your Papa goes out!' I would push him vigorously out of the door — which, of course, made him laugh.

Who was Gilles? A friend, who came fairly regularly, each time laden with provisions. He had very short hair plastered down with brilliantine, and a lean face that made him look a bit like a bird of prey. Maman would look worried when Gilles and Papa would go out together, as if she were afraid that Papa might run into some danger. When they left, Gilles would try to reassure Maman, saying airily to her, 'Things will work out. Don't worry, everything will be fine.'

He's the only person I remember, apart from one teacher. Papa used to take me to school, but not very often, and eventually I began to wonder whether I was being taken to school on certain days for my own safety, either because they were afraid of something or because something in particular was taking place at the apartment. I wasn't in the right class for my age, the others were older than me, and I was always given a seat near the teacher, next to her desk. I didn't do anything much. I was just given some paper and a pencil to keep me amused. Much later, I tried to find that school. In my mind's eye, I pictured a wide pavement with a porch and three worn grey stone steps. But I found myself on a narrow pavement with a high metal safety fence and no steps. And yet it seemed to tally with my memory, to be on the corner of the street where my parents lived, which was on the number 56 tramline.

Similarly, I didn't find the park where Papa once took me for a walk — although I don't know when. It had a little waterfall, stones, a lake and a donkey which I remember stroking, so I evidently did leave our apartment sometimes, but only with Papa. Papa was blond, I was blonde; was our blond hair enough to prevent our being suspected as Jews?

I'd go to the school at the corner of the street, clutching Papa's hand. This expedition never started smoothly. I'd refuse to leave Maman, and cling to her furiously with stubborn determination. Papa virtually had to drag me out of the door, and then I would trot along sulkily at his side. When we arrived, Papa would hand me over to the teacher, a tall woman with wavy hair, wearing an overall. She'd lead me to my seat near her and I would scrawl some pictures. I imitated Maman, drawing faces with enormous eyes.

At recess, I found myself back in the playground where, sitting beneath a tree, I'd count the leaves on the ground. It must have been autumn. When the bell rang for the end of break, the teacher would have to come and find me. I never wanted to go back inside.

During lessons, someone occasionally came in and whispered in the teacher's ear. This happened at least twice. The teacher calmly stood up, telling the children to be quiet and wait for her. She gently took me by the hand and led me to a storeroom full of school equipment. I can still hear her telling me, 'Be a good girl and stay here. We'll play a game. I'm going to shut the door, but you must be as quiet as a mouse. When I come and fetch you, I'll give you a sweet if you've been very good.' After a long time, she would come back. 'Good girl. You played that game well.' I was then given my sweet.

I didn't realise she was taking me to that pitch-black cupboard to hide me, and I was never scared, but then I've never been frightened of the dark like some children. On the contrary, I was waiting for my delicious sweet! It was such a rare treat for me. I think the only times I ever ate sweets as a child were when I emerged from that little storeroom.

I presume those were the times when

someone came to the school to check up on the children who were there. It was wartime, but I had only a very vague idea of what that meant. When Papa talked about it, Maman signalled to him to talk in German or Yiddish, so I couldn't understand. Still, I overheard them talking in French about people who had 'stayed behind'. But stayed where? In Poland, Germany or Russia? I think I may have heard them talking about Maman's family. She said that she was worried and Papa replied, 'We couldn't. They didn't want to come.'

I also overheard some snippets of conversation between Papa and his friend Gilles. The Germans were undoubtedly the 'baddies'. Papa also talked about the star which the Jews were supposed to wear and which, he said, he would never put on. I often wondered what he did during the day. He worked for a time at the Town Hall and he once brought back a towel. But that job didn't last long. There was also the rifle hidden in a cupboard on the landing. I saw it once and I heard Maman say something to my father — she was worried that I'd seen it. Did Papa belong to a resistance network with Gilles?

As for Maman, she lit candles and said prayers. She sang, sewed, drew and let me play on my own under the bed, where I had an entire imaginary menagerie at my disposal, an army made up of all kinds of animals who defended me against the enemy. I was in my cave, the entrance guarded by a cobra; other snakes led the attack, the tigers obeyed me, the wolves followed me, the elephant lifted me on to his back with his trunk, the birds of prey circled in the sky and the enemy were very afraid. I conquered them, then meted out justice. The defeated enemy grovelled at my feet. I played at my little war for hours, and if Maman bent over to see what I was doing with a smile on her face, I'd say firmly, 'Don't disturb me, Maman. I'm playing!'

I didn't want her to hear me telling my stories or talking to the tigers or the snakes. I was powerful. I commanded my troops in an unreal world which was completely real to me. The tiger was the strongest, as it could kill with a swipe of its claws, the elephant trampled the enemy or tossed them into the air and the snakes poisoned everyone. My war was deadly serious and very effective: the enemy disappeared as if by magic. Naturally, the enemy was always German.

Papa taught me about military strategy using clothes pegs. We played with them as if we were playing chess. He had his troops and I had mine, arranged in small groups on the table. Both of us had our divisions, and the idea was to find a way through in order to surround the enemy and emerge the overall winner. Although I didn't realise it then, the only games I played were concerned with warfare, whether it was under the bed in my imaginary cave or on the table with clothes-peg troops. I was a little soldier without a uniform, bursting with energy which Maman found very hard to control. On occasion, I would run across the room in all directions, jumping and leaping like my tigers, despite not being allowed to make any noise on the wooden floor. I found it difficult and frustrating to keep quiet all the time. I wasn't unhappy, apart from about being shut inside all day. But I needed to show my feelings so badly that I sometimes put on my shoes to make a noise deliberately. I usually walked around the apartment in bare feet or wearing ankle socks. Maman panicked at the slightest noise. She would seize hold of my shoulders, her dark eyes boring into mine: 'Mishke! Try to understand! You mustn't do that.'

I could sense her fear of an invisible danger and thought it was terribly unfair. Everything was grey and colourless, except Maman. I longed for colour, longed to eat, longed to make some noise, longed to shake up this

24

dreary, silent life. Instead of shouting, though, I whispered as I played and, instead of sweets and other treats, I slurped down my spoonfuls of cod-liver oil while Maman wrinkled up her lovely nose and laughed. I would have done anything in the world to see her laugh. I loved it when she washed me in the huge basin and I hated it when Papa put his arms round her. I snuggled up to her, surrounded by her smell. At night, the three of us slept in the same bed, with me in the middle. It wasn't very warm, but I was snug between Papa and Maman. I would locate her earlobe and rub it between two fingers to help me fall asleep, until it became hot and Maman offered me the other one, which was nice and cool. Papa didn't like this ritual: 'Are you going to let her do that until she's married?'

But Maman didn't stop me and it was wonderful to fall asleep like that, my nose buried in her long hair. I was safe from everything, cradled by love, cocooned by the lily of the valley fragrance of Maman's hair. I didn't ever want to leave her. I could have spent my whole life in that shabby apartment, with no furniture and coats hanging on the doors, listening to Maman singing me a lullaby or telling me stories in her delightful Russian-tinged accent. She was my home.

She showed me life, her small light brushes painting faces or flowers in pastel colours, her slender hands mending clothes. The lace shawl she wore for praying. The notebook in which she jotted mysterious things — 'No, Mishke, don't touch that. It belongs to Maman. It contains little secrets that no one else knows.'

Maman's little secrets were safe from anyone who couldn't read Russian. She wrote them in a small, elegant hand in a notebook which had a red cover with a black and gold pattern. She kept it with an envelope stuffed with notes. I knew what money looked like, although I didn't know what it was used for. No one gave me any and I didn't go anywhere; nor did Maman. I don't know if Papa had earned the money at work or if it was a sum put by in case of danger. Maman kept it carefully locked in a box. Papa hadn't worked for a long time, perhaps for several months — I found it difficult to keep track of time. I know only that it wasn't long before everything ran short. Maman didn't often take money out of that envelope. Gilles provided the basic essentials when it came to food and we made do with that.

I don't remember being very hungry, even if we often ate the same food in small quantities. The few times when Papa dragged me to school are the only bad memories I have of this period in my life. The first time, I almost howled on the staircase of our building. Papa sensed it and put his hand over my mouth. 'You mustn't say a word! You must be quiet!' His blue eyes bored into me. He didn't usually speak to me like that. I realised he was referring to that invisible danger and I bit my lip and quickly followed him downstairs. Out in the street, he said, 'You're always asking to go out — well, now you're outside and you must be quiet. I'm taking you to a place where you'll have some fun.'

I was a little frightened by the street, and he was striding along quickly. I had the impression that they had just come to a decision about me, perhaps because I was becoming unruly at home and making too much noise. But I didn't feel comfortable outside. I'd been cooped up in that apartment with my mother for too long. We had almost certainly lived somewhere else before. I seem to recall playing in a courtyard or a small garden. I remember some flowers, a circular flowerbed, and I can vaguely see myself running around it. I must have attended some local school, learned the alphabet, then words and numbers, because I could count on my fingers and read and write a little — but who had taught me? Most people remember a schoolteacher from when they were that age, but I don't. My memories begin with that apartment and are filled only with Jules and Maman and the school at the corner of the street. Before that, there is nothing but a black hole. As though I was born at the age of six.

Once I'd been handed over to the teacher, Papa kissed me and gazed deep into my eyes to make it clear that he wasn't abandoning me. 'I'll come and get you. Don't forget. I'll collect you.' From his pocket he took a little pencil case shaped like a dog, and gave it to me. It contained two or three pencils and an eraser. The teacher took me to a classroom where I was the only small child. The other children didn't bat an eyelid at my arrival, as if they had been warned beforehand. They didn't show any interest in me but just carried on working and playing together. Sitting on the ground in the playground, I counted the leaves, and I did the same the next four or five times I went.

A certain amount of time elapsed between each trip to school. The second time I was determined not to go; the memory of my separation from Maman was too fresh, and Papa had to resort to persuasion: Maman was tired, she needed to rest and I had to put up with it in order to make her happy. I'm not easily swayed by persuasion. I was, and still am, very stubborn. I promised anything as long as he didn't make me go out. I wouldn't move, I'd sit on the chair all day, I wouldn't bounce on the bed, I wouldn't run in the room. Finally, tired of the fighting, Maman said, 'Let her stay.'

I regained the safety and darkness of my cave under the bed with my snakes and tigers. I wasn't afraid of them. No one had ever taught me to be scared of wolves or bears or eagles. Animals were my real clan, even though I had seen them only in pictures. I knew that they really existed 'in the forest', that they drank in rivers and lakes and ate prey, but their way of life didn't seem at all frightening. My mind wasn't filled with childish fears. I didn't know any children or any other adults, and if the fox chased the rabbit or the lion hunted a doe in the little books my parents gave me, it was just to eat, and I thought that was perfectly normal. A hen scratched about with her chicks, a bitch slept with her puppies and I slept with Maman. I was an animal like them. To be more precise, the idea of a 'wild' animal never crossed my mind. I was more inclined to believe that men were 'wild, German and wicked'. They had started the war, so we had to fight them and stand up to them. Animals didn't create those types of problem. On the contrary, they were on my side when I played my favourite game.

The reason I was so isolated during my childhood was that Papa was a German Jew and Maman was a native Russian Jew and they had almost certainly fled to Belgium when the pogroms began in Germany. Now that Belgium was under German occupation, they were forced to go into hiding. If my assumption is correct — and I can't see any other interpretation — Gilles must have belonged to a network assigned to help us. Papa had told me the story of a little girl called Rachel who had been very stupid. She had said to someone — the grocer, I think — 'My name isn't the same as Papa's any more. My name is . . . '

I don't remember the rest. It must have been a name like Dupont or Durand. In any case, the little girl and her parents were taken away by the police, and Papa obviously wanted to make it quite clear that I wasn't to talk about my parents. It was after this story that Maman taught me a new rule. I already knew that my name was just Mishke, without any surname. This was so ingrained that I still don't know anything about my parents' identities, except their first names. The new rule added that if someone came to fetch me instead of Papa, saying, 'Are you Mishke? Come with me,' I was to answer 'Yes' and go with that person without making a fuss. 'Is that clear? Your name is Mishke and you do as you're told. Don't worry, it'll probably never happen, unless Papa is running late. Is that clear? Tell me you understand — do you? This is very serious, Mishke. Repeat it back to me!'

I had to say that I understood perfectly several times and even promise I'd do as I was told to please her, even though I didn't understand the meaning of this new rule. As far as I was concerned, someone was just going to take me home to Maman and, anyway, it would probably never happen. On the other hand, if anyone had asked my name for some reason, I wouldn't have been able to answer anything other than 'Mishke', which could pass as a typical diminutive in Brussels — people were called Deniske, Pierrettke — and, in any case, was derived from Belgian French since that was the only language I'd ever spoken and understood. Papa spoke German and French equally fluently, unlike Maman, whose accent could be spotted immediately. That must have been why she stayed at home with me all the time.

I'll never forget that day in 1941 when I left

her to go to that wretched school, not knowing that I'd never see her again. I still blame myself for not studying her face more closely or breathing in the fragrance of her hair for longer. If I had known, though, they would have had to tear me limb from limb to get me away from her. Her face has blurred with time and all I have left now is her hair, which was so long that she sometimes put it up in a bun, her gentle voice, a gaily patterned dress, a forgotten song that I can't even hum any more and a few Russian words that she lovingly taught me. I'll never know what they did with her hair in the place she was taken to. I would have liked to stay with her, to live or die by her side. She wanted to save me, but I didn't want to be saved.

Before letting go of my hand, Papa had told me again that he would be collecting me. I'd spent the break sitting under my tree, looking at the buildings on the other side of the school wall, imagining that Maman was out there somewhere and could see me. I was now sitting on my own on the three worn stone steps under the porch. Usually the teacher kept me company until Papa took my hand again for the walk home. This time, though, I couldn't see the teacher. I think she'd said he wouldn't be long and then left me by myself. Time passed and I watched the street. The school door was closed, so I invented a game while I was waiting. I would shut my eyes and count to fifteen, and then Papa would arrive. Because he still wasn't there when I reached fifteen, I started over — and again, and again. I was still counting when a voice said, 'Are you Mishke? Come with me.'

At first I was surprised; then I remembered Maman's instructions. She'd made me promise to do as I was told, so I did. I hadn't seen the woman approaching, probably because I was busy counting. She was dumpy and old, her voice rather harsh, and she was wearing a black coat and headscarf. She took me by the hand, saying, 'Come on, then.'

I followed her mechanically. We walked back to the corner of the street where my parents lived and suddenly there was a great deal of noise, shouting, trucks and crowds of people. It looked as though they were fighting or as though some of them were hitting others. The woman made me cross the road quickly, saying, 'Don't look, Mishke.' She pulled me along by the hand, repeating, 'Don't look, Mishke.' Every time she said my name, I thought about Maman. I thought she was taking me to her and that I was going to be reunited with my parents.

Everything was unfamiliar now. Much

further on, we came to a tram stop where we waited for a while; the woman didn't say a word. We climbed into a yellow tram. There was a man with a large bag selling tickets and shouting continually in French and Flemish, '*Tout le monde est servi? Allemon bediend?*' The woman paid and made me sit next to her, advising me to be quiet.

In a whisper, I asked, 'Where are we going?'

'Shhh. You'll see.'

The tram continued along its route and I watched the unfamiliar streets roll past. Although I had gazed at the tramline on the way to school before, this was the first time I'd ridden in the little tram. The woman in black didn't say anything to explain what was happening or to reassure me. She was on edge. There were German soldiers in the tram, apparently passengers like us; they weren't speaking to anyone. I looked at the cars, the people walking in the street, everything I'd never had the opportunity to see before. The tram stopped at the end of what seemed a very long journey and the conductor shouted, '*Terminus!*'

From what I was able to piece together later, we'd stopped at the Rond-point du Meir, taking what was then the number 56 tram in the direction of Schaerbeek. This neighbourhood seemed like a different country. I could see trees and it was very quiet. The woman led me down a path running alongside a park, then along a lane, then down an even narrower alleyway which brought us out in front of a church. From there, we walked along a dark, bleak street. She was walking very fast and sometimes I dragged my feet a little, but then I would force my pace to match hers at the thought of seeing Maman again.

The houses there were low and narrow. We walked alongside what might have been a factory wall, which was tall, grey and very long. The woman stopped in front of one of the narrow houses and went inside, pulling me after her by the hand. I clearly remember going up two steps to reach a landing, then down five or six others into a room below, whose window was level with the street we had just walked along. This was a dining room with an adjoining kitchen. There were two cupboards, neatly arranged table and chairs and, on the far side of the room, a large wood-burning stove. I thought that the rest of the house must be upstairs. I could just glimpse a staircase at the end of a corridor with clothes hanging on the wall and shoes lined up in rows on the floor. There were two armchairs.

Everything was clean and tidy, imposing and unwelcoming, like the tall woman who suddenly appeared before us. Her wavy hair, which was a surprising mauvish white, was swept back off her face. She opened a thin mouth, revealing gold teeth. Her face, which was both stern and ridiculous, frightened me. Curtly, she said, 'Is everything arranged?'

'Yes.' The woman in black took an envelope from her bag and handed it to her.

The woman with mauve hair checked the contents. I glimpsed some notes. She pointed to an armchair: 'Sit down over there.' I wondered what I was doing here and especially where Maman was. The armchair was nice, not tattered or threadbare like the one in our apartment where Maman would sit to sew.

The woman in black was leaving without any further explanation. She barely glanced in my direction before she left, saying, 'Good luck.'

I was left on my own with the woman with mauve hair, who, without moving from the kitchen, called to someone, 'Janine!' She then addressed me for the second time: 'Janine will show you to your room. Change into the clothes on the bed.'

'What about Maman and Papa?'

'We don't talk about that here. Get that

36

into your head. We don't talk about that here.' The thin mouth had issued an order that was not to be disobeyed. She hadn't even smiled and hadn't come near me. If she had, I was so scared of her that I think I'd have run away as fast as my legs would carry me.

Feeling completely bewildered, with no explanations or reason for hope, I allowed myself be led away in silence by Janine, a red-faced maid with short hair and an imposing figure, who spoke Flemish and jabbered a little French. She took me upstairs to another landing, where I was shown a windowless boxroom behind a curtain. There was a bed, with some clothes laid out on the blanket — a dark skirt and a blouse with a tight buttoned collar, which she signalled I should put on. The maid took away my dog pencil case and said, in strongly accented French, 'They're waiting for you downstairs for dinner.'

I felt such a strong urge to cry that I sobbed for a long time, sitting alone on that bed. I'd lost my parents and the maid had taken away the only thing I possessed. My life as a cherished little girl had come to an end that day in the house of that woman with mauve hair, who didn't like me. She had accepted the money, but I wasn't welcome and she was going to make sure I knew it. It was obvious, although I didn't know it then, that my parents had been rounded up and that this rescue plan had been in place for some time. Why they chose that particular woman was a mystery that took me years to unravel. She was married to a dentist whose uncle owned a farm not far from them. This uncle, whom I later — along with everyone else in the vicinity — called Grandpère, had worked at the Town Hall, like Gilles and Papa. This connection had probably enabled them to come up with that particular fallback solution for me, sending me to those people in exchange for a sum of money intended for my upkeep. However, if my parents had met that woman, they would never have placed me in her care.

After the war, we found out how they rescued children whose parents were in danger of being captured by the Germans. Members of secret Jewish organisations, Communists, Catholics, even members of the aristocracy were involved. These people forged Belgian identity papers for Jewish children. One trick they sometimes used was to give them the administrative identity of Belgian children whose death hadn't been registered. Other papers were forged from new documents. Around five thousand children are thought to have been saved from the camps in this way. But it was possible only if you had access to the administrative machinery, like Gilles, Papa and Grandpère.

No one ever gave me any details about the origin of my new identity. I was called Monique straight away. I was no longer seven, but four, which was very plausible, given my small size. My birthday was 12 May 1937 and I was supposed to be the daughter of the woman with mauve hair. Mishke no longer existed. My parents, Gerusha and Reuven, may have been captured in the round-up that I'd seen from a distance.

One day, Grandpère said, in front of me, 'They arrested forty men and one woman.' What woman? Maman? Why only one woman and forty men? Was it that particular round-up or another? He didn't give any details and he probably didn't know any, so I never found out what became of my parents. At that time, as I lay on my bed sobbing in that airless boxroom, I believed they were still alive and I didn't understand anything. I just felt a gaping hole and that hole is the only thing in my whole life that has ever frightened me and caused recurring nightmares. Maman had vanished into that hole and it was an unbearable feeling. It has caused me a great deal of anguish throughout my life as a survivor.

2

Lessons in Hate

The table was laid when I came down to the kitchen, and I'd dried my tears. It's hard for an adult to describe how a seven-year-old child could control such strong emotions. After sobbing my heart out, I'd suddenly decided not to cry in front of these strangers. That woman had greeted me with such contempt and they had unceremoniously taken away my pencil case, the only link I had with my parents.

The table was spread with a cloth and laden with beautiful plates and a great deal of food, dishes I'd never eaten before. There was bread and vegetables and, best of all, a dish I recognised later as roast chicken and also some caramel-coloured pieces of meat, which were actually pork chops. I'd had no experience of such an abundance of food. That feast was a revelation for a hungry little girl. I had never had so much to eat with my parents and I didn't even know that you could have such a large quantity of food at one meal. At home, we had always had the same: bread, sometimes with a little jam when Gilles brought it, and, occasionally, a piece of very salty, dried fish, which made me terribly thirsty. The rest of the time Maman cooked potatoes or cabbage, but very rarely meat. I love meat and I felt like bolting it all down.

The maid showed me to a chair and I sat waiting by myself on one side of the table, opposite the others whom I hadn't yet met: a man and a teenage boy. No one spoke to me. They were both, like me, waiting in silence.

The plates were very beautiful, with coloured rims, royal blue encircled by two gold bands. The napkins were white and neatly folded, the fabric crisp and clean. The woman with mauve hair walked in and took her seat at the head of the table, like a queen. She looked at me and said, suiting her actions to her words, 'We put our napkin on our lap.' I did as I was told and she began serving the man who, I realised, was her husband, then the teenager, her son. 'Do you want vegetables, Léopold?'

She served them slowly, offering them each a piece of everything, and it seemed to take for ever. Finally she granted me a thigh, which looked very small. So small that with hind-sight I still wonder whether it was from a chicken or a pigeon. I picked it up with my fingers and started gnawing at it. She heaved an enormous sigh as if to say, 'what on earth is that girl doing?' I glanced at her son, who sneered at me scornfully, but I couldn't have cared less because that scrap of meat felt so good in my stomach.

'Didn't anyone ever teach you to eat with a knife and fork?'

'Er . . .'

There had been none of that at home. I don't remember using a knife and fork to cut up meat. I think Papa had a pocket knife and Maman had several cooking utensils and spoons for the soup. There hadn't been any meat most of the time and if Gilles brought some once or twice, it disappeared in the soup. But I didn't have time to come up with an explanation and it would have been very hard to put into words. There wasn't much I could do with a chicken thigh, anyway, except gnaw it.

'Where was the girl brought up? Wipe your mouth!' That woman never saw any good in me. She always subjected me to spiteful remarks and it started straight away with that first meal. I swallowed the scrap of chicken and looked at the rest of the dish with an expression that provoked another scornful remark: 'You want some more meat, do you? What a surprise!' As if it were too much to ask! But I said yes anyway and was given that wonderful caramel-coloured meat. It was delicious. I must have said so, because she replied, 'Delicious! Of course it's delicious. It's a pork chop!' And she and her son began to laugh, apparently well pleased by some joke that I didn't understand until much later. Jews don't eat pork.

Her husband didn't say a word. He was quiet, unassuming and rather lost in his thoughts. In any case, he seemed strangely detached from his wife and son. It didn't appear to matter to him that there was someone else at his table. Once the meal was finished, he disappeared and I was ordered up to my room. The maid had a real bedroom with a window, furniture and a bed covered with floral fabric. My boxroom behind the curtain was clearly used only to put people up on a spare bed.

The hardest thing for me to bear in that hostile environment was the silence about my parents. That woman had considered it far more important to dine on time than to take a few minutes to comfort me and simply tell me why I was there, what decisions had been made about me. When I was on my own that

43

night, I cried so much that the next morning the maid complained that she had not been able to sleep a wink because 'That kid was crying!'

The woman with mauve hair finally spoke to me. 'Listen to me. You'll have to get used to this. You live here now and you should be glad! Stop making such a fuss about it!'

'But I want to see Papa and Maman.'

'I'm your mother now and you will call me Maman!'

She'd touched such a sensitive nerve that I was left speechless. I wouldn't have called her Maman for anything. How dare that dreadful woman compare herself to my beautiful Maman? What right did she have? If only she had at least explained that it was a necessary lie to protect my new position as a refugee in her house. If only she had told me, 'You're in danger because you're Jewish. Your parents have been arrested and they've asked me to look after you until they come back one day.' Instead, I took the order in the spirit it was given — very badly and with a great deal of spite. I said to myself, 'No way! I'll never call you Maman!' And although I didn't say it out loud, I kept my word, which infuriated her.

If Grandpère, his wife Marthe and his farm hadn't come into my life fairly soon after that, I wouldn't have been able to stay with

44

that woman. I would have gone anywhere, anyhow and with nothing. It was needlessly cruel to try to make me call her Maman when I was still mourning the loss of my mother.

I gave it a great deal of thought later in life and I still wondered why that woman had taken me in. The only explanation was the envelope I'd seen change hands. Grandpère once mentioned a sum of 75,000 francs. I'd like to know how much 75,000 Belgian francs in 1941 would be worth today, to gain an idea what the true value was to her of an undesirable commodity like me.

After issuing that directive, she sent me off to have breakfast. The previous evening, despite everything, I'd eaten more than I'd ever eaten before and if the atmosphere hadn't been so unpleasant I would have enjoyed it even more, because it was so delicious. That morning, I was greeted by the sight of golden bread and jam. I was given a slice of bread which I spread thickly with an enormous spoonful of red jam. Her son sniggered when his mother snatched it out of my hands and scraped off the jam with a knife, leaving only the thinnest film.

That morning I was in a state of shock. My heart was so heavy that if I'd spoken, I would have burst into tears and I didn't want to do that in front of that horrible woman. Call her

Maman? Watch her snatch the jam out of my mouth? Hatred suddenly flared up in my heart and swept over me.

I would have liked to strangle her, and I think I could have done it. I wanted to hit her, stamp on her feet, kick her legs, anything I could manage, given my size. This feeling of sudden, violent hatred often overtook me after that. I knew I mustn't react, but I also knew that I could, and that made me feel better. So I gazed at her, and in my mind's eye I pulled out her gold teeth one by one, I strangled her, I chopped off her ugly head with its crown of mauve hair. It all happened in my imagination, in silence. I wanted to strip her down to her ugliness and spitefulness, so that she would no longer have the power to hurt me. Compared with that woman, Maman was the sun, her thick perfumed hair was a dense, floating aureole, a delicate, undulating cloud. Ever since then, every time I've eaten jam, I've spread a really thick layer of it on my bread.

'Where on earth were you brought up? Answer me! No one eats like that!'

'Sorry . . .'

'Sorry, who?'

'Sorry, Madame.'

'Not Madame. You will call me Maman.'

'No, Madame.'

'That girl is as stubborn as a mule! What is to be done with her?'

No one would do anything. She'd taken me in for the money. I was a burden and would continue to be one. I never called her Maman and, after a time, she gave up trying to force me.

But I asked where my parents were on several occasions and each time she gave the same answer. 'We don't talk about that! I'm taking you to have some photos done. From now on, your name is Monique and you're four years old.'

'Why am I four years old?'

'Don't ask stupid questions. You're Monique Valle and you're four years old. Try and get that into your head.'

Mishke, my name was Mishke. I didn't care whether I was four or seven, but 'Monique' . . .

After tying a ridiculous bow on my head, she dragged me by the hand into a photographer's studio. It wasn't going to take long, but she complained on the way that she had better things to do with her time. She had nothing to do, though. Orders to give to the maid to cook this or that. A little sewing. When she sat down at her sewing machine, she made me sit on the floor on a cushion and gave me work to do: unpick this, learn

47

how to overstitch a hem, chores that bored me silly.

During the day, I saw virtually no one except her and the maid. Her dentist husband disappeared into his surgery and put in an appearance only at mealtimes, when he hardly spoke. On one occasion, he examined my teeth and concluded that they were very strong. I had no idea what her son did during the day, but I didn't care. I had thought he was just a boy but in fact he must have been around eighteen or twenty and he seemed as stupid as his mother, with whom he always agreed — 'Yes, Maman, no, Maman.' He laughed at me as soon as she mocked me. She often called me a 'Boeotian'.

I learned the definition of that word a long time later. The Boeotians lived in Greece. They were renowned in antiquity for their music, poetry and all kinds of science. They were also powerful soldiers and governed Greece until the reign of Alexander the Great. When I discovered this, I told myself that she was the philistine for making such a stupid mistake when she was trying to belittle me.

One day, one of her relatives, a woman called Fernande, came to see her. They were speaking in whispers, obviously about me. I listened. She said, 'I couldn't care less if she went, but if I had to lose Janine, I'd shed bitter tears of blood.' I pictured those tears of blood trickling down her face.

Several days later, I was taken to the farm to see her husband's uncle. At last she'd found a use for me: her precious son Léopold would no longer have to traipse there and back to fetch their provisions.

Léopold came with me the first time to show me the way and introduce me to Grandpère as the new messenger. When we arrived, the man was very surly, barely civil. He obviously didn't like his great-nephew. He spoke a few words to him, then lost no time in addressing me: 'You! Come with me! I want to show you something!' Léopold made as if to follow us and he said, 'No, you can stay here.'

Grandpère showed me round the farm. He showed me the dogs, the pigs, the hens and the Malines cuckoo. I learned that the Malines cuckoo was a black and white speckled hen. She was pretty and I was even allowed to touch her.

He softened when he saw how happy I was. 'Well now, *petite*, you're not going to break the eggs when you come to collect them, are you?'

'No, I'll be very careful.'

'Good. Things will work out fine, then!'

Then he said to Léopold, 'You can send her. There won't be a problem. All *she* has to do is give her the list.'

He said '*she*' as if he didn't want anything to do with his nephew's wife. He obviously wasn't too fond of her. It was the farm who fed her. All those lovely things on her table, despite the war, came from Grandpère Ernest and his wife Marthe. It was they who provided her with butter, milk and cheese and gave her vegetables, mutton, chicken and pork.

The farm seemed huge to me. The farmhouse was a solid building with spacious rooms and there was a great deal of land. Grandpère did all the work, helped only by his wife.

If he wasn't very keen on old mauve-hair, she felt exactly the same way about him. She was a Catholic, he was a non-believer; she was middle-class, he was left-wing. Referring to his anti-Church stance, she'd call him a '*bouffeur de curé*' — and he did tend to caw like a crow whenever he saw a black-coated priest. I thought it was funny. He was gruff, warm-hearted and alive. The others were already dead, devoid of the slightest kindness or compassion. It wasn't long before I heard Grandpère mocking her, calling her names like 'bigot' and 'the Virago'. Her name was

50

actually Marguerite. The nickname Virago appealed to me and I'd privately use it for her. I'd call her 'Madame' out loud, but 'the Virago' in my head. Something in the sound of the word suited her down to the ground. Grandpère also said, 'She's a thief!'

I didn't know what she'd stolen but she was a thief! He never had anything good to say to her on the rare occasions she did come to the farm. One day he made me laugh when he opened the door to her: 'Oh, is that you? I didn't recognise you! I thought it was someone wearing a hat!' All that could be seen through his opaque glazed door was the newcomer's outline, and Grandpère was obliquely making fun of her helmet of mauve hair. She pursed her thin lips even more tightly when he made fun of her openly, but she didn't reply. It was a strange family with secrets I didn't understand, but they didn't matter much to me once Grandpère was part of my life.

Grandpère Ernest had a magnificent, beautifully rounded amber pipe. I told him how much I liked it and he replied, 'This is my favourite, though,' showing me an old hexagonal wooden pipe, which was much shorter. 'Old, seasoned pipes are the best, you know.'

My job was to bring back provisions from

the farm as quickly as possible, but I began spending longer and longer at the farm, which infuriated the Virago: 'You're wasting time! At what time do you think we'll eat if we don't get the meal ready?'

I kept quiet about the things Grandpère and I did at the farm. I was so happy there. He taught me all kinds of things. I could climb a ladder, jump in the hay, play with the dogs, Ita and Rita, and eat fruit and the pies that Marthe baked.

Marthe made me some clothes so that I could play in comfort, without the skirt and starchy blouse that the Virago made me wear. I was a real tomboy, and Marthe was worried I'd break something, but Grandpère said, 'Bah! She'll be fine! It does her good to play! Leave her be!'

'Yes, but wearing that skirt . . . '

So Marthe made me a little pair of baggy trousers to wear under a skirt of the same fabric. She also made some little white blouses with short sleeves. They looked pretty and I was comfortable, but there was such a fuss when I went back in that outfit. 'What on earth have you got on? What *has* she got you wearing?'

The Virago confiscated my baggy trousers. Marthe said it didn't matter and that she'd make me some more that I could wear just on

52

the farm. Grandpère grumbled about 'that Marguerite', who deserved to have been sent packing from the farm a thousand times over. 'She's just out for what she can get, she's a poisonous . . . I told her one day never to set foot in here again and since then she's sent her son and now you. All she wants is her supplies. This family, *mon petit coco*, is like *Wuthering Heights*!'

I imagined Marguerite and her son standing on the heights in the howling wind. Obviously I didn't read the book until later, but it was clear to me that this family had a long history filled with acts of wickedness and revenge. Grandpère had no time for human beings in general. I can still hear him saying, 'Beasts are better than men. Beasts mean you no harm. They are grateful. You'll never see an animal waging war. An animal kills only for food. Humans kill for any reason, not just for food.'

That was how Grandpère passed on his philosophy of the world and nature. Watching a simple ant carrying a piece of debris or examining a dead mouse with him helped me to understand the eternal cycle of things. Animals and humans died and were put in the ground. There they were eaten by worms, and the worms left behind what was needed to make the grass and trees grow, which then nourished other animals and other humans who were born. Then one day they died in their turn and it all started again.

'Do you understand? Nature is a continuous circle. And when someone dies, all you have to do is think about them to renew the circle, so they're always in your thoughts and they're not dead.' As a result of what he told me, I felt that death was nothing serious and could see how everything continually began again, so I understood why Grandpère didn't need to talk about his son.

He didn't have any children now. He and Marthe had had one son, Joseph, who had died very young, which was a great tragedy. Sometimes Marthe called me Joseph, particularly when I was playing a little too boisterously for her liking, jumping from the top of the ladder in the barn on to the pile of hay. 'Joseph, be careful.' 'Joseph, don't do that.' 'Joseph, come here.'

Grandpère told me all about it, and added, 'She was heartbroken when he died. She thinks about him often. If you don't mind, pretend you haven't noticed, and answer when she calls you Joseph.'

'It's better than Monique. I don't like it. Why am I called Monique?'

'Monique comes from a Greek word meaning 'alone'. It's not a bad name for you.

You are alone. And, anyway, it's necessary as a precaution. Do you understand? As a precaution. Names don't matter. I call you '*mon petit coco*', you call me Grandpère, and Marthe calls you Joseph, because she thinks about him. Everyone has their own reason for the names they call other people. Personally, the name I give that nasty piece of work Hitler, who's poisoning the world, is 'the painter and decorator' because he's not a soldier, he's a madman who wants to repaint the world in his own colour. But his colour isn't beautiful, it's *vert-de-gris*, greyish green, like the uniforms. As for you, *mon petit coco*, we call you Monique as a precaution, because we don't want you to come to any harm.'

Doing things 'as a precaution' was an expression my parents had used, so I understood it. We hadn't been allowed to make any noise, as a precaution; we hadn't been able to go out, as a precaution; so the present precaution of calling me Monique had something to do with my parents. That was how I understood it and, anyway, I always thought of myself as Mishke.

'Joseph, you're filthy! Come and wash in the basin!' I had become a surrogate Joseph. Marthe never mentioned him to me, but sometimes I caught a glimpse of little Joseph's photo in her glasses case. A boy, not

55

yet a young man, wearing a sailor suit, with a belt and sabre. The photo was old and a little yellowed and it was strange to see that unknown boy, by whose name I was sometimes called, appear and disappear when she opened or closed her glasses case with a click. That was the circle of nature.

I think Grandpère was glad that Marthe was taking care of me. He thought I was good for her. How old would she have been? She seemed very old to me, but she may only have been about forty. Grandpère was older, but he always held himself as stiff as a poker, and he was strong and tall with a bushy moustache. I dared to ask him where my parents were. 'They were arrested, *mon petit coco*.' Arrested . . . I didn't really understand what that meant, so he added, 'The Germans captured them and took them away with them. The filthy *Boches* are evil men, *ma petite*. Never forget that.'

'But the *Boches* have children. Are they evil too?'

'Evil begets evil. Never go anywhere near them. Everything they do is evil.'

'Where did they take my parents?'

'They took them back to their country, in the East.'

I asked where the East was, and the lessons began. Grandpère brought out an old geography book, with colour maps, which may once have belonged to Joseph, and he explained where the cardinal points were on the map of pre-war Europe. France was blue, Belgium golden-yellow, Germany green, Italy orange, and so on. Grandpère patiently helped me read the names of the big cities, starting with those in Belgium, then Germany, Poland, Russia, and so on. He showed me the borders on the map, with war raging everywhere.

'The East is here, you see. That's Germany, and Russia is even further east. On the other side is the West. You can't go wrong. If you open your arms wide, you can say that your right arm is to your east and your left arm is to your west. Your head is north and your feet are south.'

When I traced across the differently coloured countries with my finger on the map, the East looked quite close. So that's where Maman was, somewhere in the dark green, not too far from the yellow. I asked Grandpère if he knew Maman and he replied quickly, 'You have pretty ears, just like her. But don't dwell on it too much, *mon petit coco*, otherwise you'll get upset.'

Grandpère taught me geography in his own way. I learned to say 'potato' in German. He had lived in Germany before the war, and according to him, the Germans, the 'filthy *Boches*', always stood stiff as ramrods and ate only potatoes and sauerkraut. The Belgians were crafty buggers who always managed to get round the law, especially if it was a *Boche* law. You had to have a hot potato in your mouth if you wanted to speak American, the French liked wine and told funny stories, the Italians ran like rabbits and were pally with the *Boches*, while the Russians wore fur on their heads and sang and danced, and drank like fish!

Grandpère's education was founded on simple precepts: lessons about things, about geography, which I learned better with him than in school, and natural science lessons. If Ita, the male dog, wanted to make puppies with Rita, the bitch, he did it in the same way as the ram mated with the ewe. I also had sports lessons — I learned to ride a bike in the farmyard, climb trees and chase the hens — and lessons in astronomy. 'Look at the moon. You see that star over there? That's the North Star. So where's the East?'

The East held no more secrets for me, but I wanted the moon — and Grandpère laughed and pretended to give it to me. And he gave me singing lessons into the bargain:

Joli mois de mai quand reviendras-tu
M'apporter des feuilles, m'apporter des
  feuilles . . .
Joli mois de mai quand reviendras-tu
M'apporter des feuilles pour torcher
  mon cul . . .

Lovely month of May when will you
  return
To bring me leaves, bring me leaves . . .
Lovely month of May when will you
  return
And bring me leaves to wipe my
  arse . . .

So he also taught me to laugh. But the Virago didn't like us spending so much time together. She suspected that Marthe wanted to turn me into a bad girl because one day Marthe dressed me up as a princess and painted my mouth with lipstick. She was wrong. She was sure that Grandpère was saying horrible things about her — and about that she was right.

Another lesson Grandpère taught me was not to repeat what we did or said at the farm. 'If she asks what I've been saying, you answer, 'He asked how you were.' If she asks what you did, you answer, 'I worked in the henhouse.' '

'But that's a lie!'

'There's one lesson you should learn. Bad people always use what people tell them. So if you don't want to lie to her, act stupid whenever she asks you a question and say . . . nothing! When in doubt, it's always better to keep quiet, *mon petit coco*. If you're afraid of someone, don't breathe a word. If you don't know who you're dealing with, keep your mouth shut. Talk only if you trust someone. Look at the animals: they don't speak and yet they understand each other. You'll never have a problem with them, and if you listen carefully you'll also understand them.'

The days spent with Grandpère were very full and I was eager to learn everything he could teach me. All I had known before, with no school and nothing interesting to do, was emptiness, silence and confinement, so I soaked up this simple education.

Without my realising it, these lessons taught me to survive on hostile soil and not to trust humans. The only people I trusted apart from my parents were Grandpère and Marthe, and, thanks to them, I didn't believe Maman and Papa were dead. They were in the East, not far from the farm. They had been 'arrested' and kept there by the war, and since Grandpère said that the *Boches* would lose the war, one day my parents would no longer be arrested and they could come and find me.

I was a strong, sturdy child. I ate my fill despite the Virago, from whom I occasionally stole jam or bread during the night after creeping stealthily downstairs. I walked a couple of miles each day to the farm to bring back baskets of vegetables, eggs and all the food that Grandpère gave his nephew. The Virago benefited from this, which was fortunate for me, since I ate at her house.

Marthe kept me fed with rhubarb tarts or cherry jam. She always had a little treat for me. Warm milk fresh from the cow as well. I would carry the pail without undue difficulty to the kitchen, where she made cheese. I had to return to the house to sleep, though, and I'd walk back with leaden feet to do as I was told, help with the housework or the sewing, and sleep in my boxroom while I dreamed of Marthe and Grandpère in the big farmhouse. I don't know how long I stayed with the Virago, or at the farm. I had lost track of time since my parents had been arrested. It must have been at least a year, at any rate.

One day, on 12 May, Grandpère gave me a bunch of flowers which looked like butterflies. They were sweet peas, and he told me, 'It's your birthday.' He often gave me little surprises, saying that it was my birthday every day. But this time, there was also a delicious pie and he maintained that it really was my birthday. According to him, and he must have known somehow, I was born on 12 May. This must have been 12 May 1941 and I had just turned seven, because Maman had told me I was born in 1934. But I'm not sure about anything. Neither the dates nor how long I spent there.

I've never forgotten that magnificent sweet-smelling bouquet. I can still see the sweet peas and the pie on the table of that large farmhouse kitchen which was filled with light. It was so bright and warm. I learned about the world on that table and I was a good pupil. What a pleasure it was to recognise some country or other, to put my finger on Italy or say the name of a town and point to where it was on the map. 'Put your finger on the map, but don't look at the name,' he'd say. 'Spell out the letters.'

Grandpère had taken over from Maman in making me recite the alphabet, write sentences and count on my fingers. I used my hand to measure things: so many hands from the ground to my head. I managed quite well for my size, although physically I was 'small'. 'But very muscular,' said Grandpère. This was his way of sizing someone up. His wife,

Marthe, was a 'big, beautiful woman', and one day I would also be a 'big, beautiful woman'. For the time being, I was still a *petit coco*, who needed to play on her own, like a boy.

I wasn't used to mixing with other children. Marthe had tried bringing home a neighbour's boy for me to play with, but we had ended up fighting and Grandpère had said, 'You should leave her be. She doesn't need or want to play with other girls or boys. She doesn't like it.'

Marthe wanted me to have contact with other people, but if she invited a little girl, I would hit her, and if it was a boy, I wanted to show I was stronger than he was. I was a loner — and I still am. I was forced to be isolated. It wasn't by choice, but I had to put up with it, first out of necessity for my parents, and then because I was on my own at the Virago's house and no one liked me, and in the end Marthe and Grandpère were the only company I wanted.

The happiest time I spent with them came about by chance. The Virago had to pay a visit to a relative, so she sent me to stay with Grandpère. Two fantastic days at the farm and, best of all, an afternoon in town with Marthe.

We walked to the start of the tramline and

sat in the tram. Marthe was wearing a pretty hat. She'd made it herself, along with the little coat and bonnet with two ribbons that I was wearing proudly. Marthe had rough hands, accustomed to working in the fields, but when she sewed she had very nimble fingers. We walked along a little street to a big square, where I looked in the shop windows. Strangely enough, this trip didn't make me anxious, even though it was the first time I'd been taken into town with all those people. With my hand in Marthe's, nothing could harm me. I stopped to look at cakes in a window and Marthe said, 'Would you like a cake? Let's buy a cake.' I'd never eaten anything like it before — and this was to be the last for a very long time. It was a tiny coffee-cream cake and it was delicious. Everything was in short supply in Belgium at that time. The cake was tiny and I have no idea what it was really made from, but I'd never seen a cake, apart from the pies at the farm, so for me it was the height of luxury.

After that treat, we went into a toyshop and Marthe bought me a doll with eyes that opened and closed. She was dressed in a baby coat with a bow around the neck, which was decorated with a scrap of lace. It was a beautiful doll and I was very proud and happy. It was the first new toy I'd had as a little girl (and the only one I was ever to have). I cradled it like a baby, and we went to catch the tram to go home. When we boarded it, there was a German soldier standing near the door; Marthe quickly walked past him to find a seat, pushing me in front of her. Naturally, I too had noticed the German. Grandpère had said to me, 'Watch out for the *vert-de-gris*,' meaning the soldiers in their greyish-green uniforms, but I wasn't worried, I was happy. Marthe said, 'You can play with your doll at home. Let her go to sleep now.'

The German went on standing motionless by the door. When we reached our stop, Marthe tried to lift me down the two steps, which were quite high, and my doll's lace snagged on the soldier's bayonet. He didn't move and it wasn't his fault. It was because Marthe had attempted to help me down. I began shouting: 'Filthy *Boche*!'

Marthe pulled me close. 'Shhh! It doesn't matter.'

I think I also shouted, 'Filthy *vert-de-gris!*' I didn't think about the danger. I don't know if the soldier understood what I was saying. He definitely saw that the doll had become caught, but he didn't say or do anything and Marthe pulled me away very fast.

On the road back to the farm, all she said was, '*Ma petite*, what you just did was very dangerous. Never ever do that again! It's very dangerous, for you, for us. You really mustn't.' She was still trembling when she told the story to Grandpère, who laughed, 'We must celebrate that! You were very brave — but you must never do it again.'

Then Marthe prepared a feast fit for a king, with meat, potatoes and spinach. It was wonderful. Grandpère told me that if I drank water after eating fried potatoes, the fat would congeal in my stomach. I stared wide-eyed and they both laughed. Marthe wasn't afraid any more. I now realise how frightened she must have been. They said something to each other which I didn't hear because they were laughing so much, and Marthe took some mustard and chased Grandpère with a spoon — she was determined to smear it over him. I was delighted by this gaiety. Life felt good.

That evening, Grandpère showed me the moon, which was round and full. The dogs were playing in the yard and refused to come in. It was a magnificent night. Marthe had given me some pyjamas which were too big for me and I was to sleep in a very soft bed with a brass bedstead, near theirs. She kissed me, saying, 'Sleep well. We had a very exciting day today.'

The next day she took me to church,

explaining that I had to go to confession to tell the priest about my sins. I'm not sure I understood why. Perhaps it was because she was herself going to confession and thought I should be doing the same as the daughter of the family, a good little Catholic. 'A sin,' explained Marthe, 'is something bad. You have to tell if you've done something bad.'

I found it entertaining. I can clearly remember the smell of the confessional and the disembodied voice, which after a long silence, because I didn't know what to say, asked me, 'Well, what have you done?'

I answered with the first thing that came into my head. 'I've done everything, except the killing!' It was Marthe who slit the hens' throats. Not me. All I did was watch and eat the chicken. I must have explained my line of reasoning to the priest, but I can't remember how. And he talked for a fairly long time afterwards. He was murmuring and obviously I didn't understand a thing, I just wanted to get out of there. When she rescued me, Marthe said, 'You were in there a long time.'

None of it meant anything to me. I knew I was Jewish, but I was also beginning to realise in my own way what my being Jewish meant in 1941 for the people around me. It was crucial not to mention it or show it because it was dangerous. It was as simple as that.

Cocooned between Marthe and Grand-père, I was blissfully unaware of many serious events. Belgium was beginning to suffer severe food shortages, the Germans were invading Russia, and during this time a nationalist called Léon Degrelle was trying to persuade the population of Brussels to fight alongside the Nazis on the Eastern Front. Grandpère read the national newspapers, which were controlled by the occupiers and were waxing lyrical about the idea. '*We are fighting*,' said that traitor Degrelle, '*for the noblest values on earth, alongside those who are liberating Europe and the world and whom Communism wanted to crush.*'

Autumn was drawing in, the *vert-de-gris* were becoming an increasingly threatening presence in our area and my cocoon was about to split wide open. When I returned to the Virago's house after that enjoyable interlude, I understood the threat. Hiding behind a door, I overheard what she was saying to one of her friends. She had just 'displayed' me to her, like a monkey in the zoo, sighing, 'You see what I've been saddled with.' I had pretended to go back to my boxroom but I was still there, waiting to hear what came next. 'When it comes down to it, if the Germans win, we'll hand her over to

68

them, and if they lose, we can always say that we did something to help her.'

I'd just had my first lessons in happiness with Grandpère and Marthe. That woman taught me all there was to know about hate.

3

Never Afraid

Although hatred may have given me the strength to hold my tongue at the Virago's house, Grandpère demonstrated the virtue of resistance by example.

Occasionally, planes would fly overhead. Shaking with terror, Marthe would take shelter in the cellar, and one day she took me with her, saying, 'Lie down on the ground!' Grandpère immediately appeared: 'Out of the question! Come on, up you get! You're coming with me. If I die, I'll die out in the open and to hell with those *Boche* bastards! They don't frighten me.'

He took me out in the garden, bellowing abuse at the planes and shaking his fist furiously as he reassured me, 'Don't be afraid. They'll drop their bombs somewhere else. We're too small to be of any interest to them. Are you afraid?'

'No.' I meant it. I believed everything he

said unreservedly. Marthe's fear was contagious and it had infected me, but his demonstration of defiance, however futile, had dispelled it.

From Grandpère I learnt to always hold my head up high and outdo myself. 'Take that log over there to Marthe.' The log was enormous, much too heavy for me, but I managed to do it by dint of sheer determination. That man exerted a considerable influence over me. He congratulated me when I learned something well and he encouraged me to tackle anything, ignoring the fact that I was a little girl.

This was quite unlike the treatment I got from the Virago, who never stopped trying to humiliate me and continually belittled my clumsy efforts to help her with her tedious sewing chores: 'What's the matter? Are you sulking? You should be grateful for what I'm doing for you. It's more than your own mother has done, believe you me!'

'That's not true! My mother gave me life.'

'Insolent girl! And where's your mother now, may I ask?'

It was such a spiteful question that I've never forgotten it. 'She' must have known where my mother was. A long way away, in any case, and with her adult powers of reasoning she must have known what was

71

happening in Belgium, since I was there, living with her, in exchange for money. How dare she say that! Admittedly I should have been grateful to her for taking me in and feeding me, but I couldn't feel grateful. And I still find it hard to write that word when I remember the look on her face as she was talking to me.

There's something about my time with those people that I'll never understand. Why was she so full of hatred for whatever or whoever had 'saddled' her with me, as she put it? Was Grandpère implicated through me? He must have been, since she hated him and he felt the same way about her. Did Grandpère force her hand in some way so that she had to let me take her name? What murky family business set them at each other's throats? It didn't make any sense. I was completely alone, surrounded by adults, without my mother, and that woman didn't show any compassion for my loneliness. I could only hate her a little more with each passing day and have nightmares every night, terrible nightmares when I would fall into the emptiness and then wake wringing with sweat with no one to comfort me. I hardened myself to it: despair kept me company at night, but during the day I tried hard to hold out, to be a rebel or a hypocrite. I looked daggers at her, I chopped her into little pieces in silence. I defended myself as best I could.

Over the weeks, our relationship went from bad to worse. She continually made remarks about my stupidity, my incompetence when it came to learning to sew or doing the housework. I didn't have a proper relationship with anyone in that house. I was in the way and her 'wonderful maid', Janine, shamelessly stripped me of my few possessions.

Grandpère gave me a small dark green wallet. It was very plain and made of imitation leather. I didn't put much in it — just a bird's feather, a pretty leaf, a pebble — but it was mine. I made the mistake of bringing it back to my boxroom, whereas usually Marthe kept all my little treasures at the farm, like my doll and an old yellow bear; she knew very well what '*l'autre*', the other, was like. Remembering the theft of my school pencil case, wanted to show that it was mine and, as I couldn't write my name on it, I bit the corner of the wallet very hard to imprint it with my tooth marks.

I was intending to hide it somewhere, but I didn't have time. I must have left the boxroom, perhaps to wash my hands, I don't remember, but when I came back upstairs a few minutes later, my wallet had gone. I felt sick. It had been a gift from Grandpère that very day.

I opened the door to Janine's bedroom and saw it lying on her bed. I ran over to claim it and she yelled, 'Hey! That's mine!'

'No, it's not! It's mine! Anyway, it has my tooth marks on it. I know it's mine.'

This didn't impress her. She continued to shout at me, then went downstairs to complain to '*l'autre*', while I ran behind her, furious.

I was sure that this time I'd be proved right. The wallet bore my mark and no one could deny it. 'It's mine! I bit it.'

'And how could you have come by this, eh? Where did it come from?'

I wanted to bite her, but I didn't reply. 'When things are going badly, don't say a word,' Grandpère used to say. 'Anything you say can always be used against you.' He may have been thinking about another kind of danger, but I obeyed his instruction to the letter.

The Virago hated him so much that if I'd said that the wallet was a gift from him, I wouldn't have been given it back anyway. And, above all, it was essential that I didn't let her know how happy I was at the farm. I was really much too afraid I'd be forbidden to go there, and it was the only place I could be free.

I was so angry, I physically ground my teeth as I stood there in front of her; she must have heard. This is a reflex I've retained all my life. Every time circumstances force me to stay quiet when I'm faced with a glaring injustice, I keep my mouth closed and my teeth protest. That day, I thought to myself, 'You wait until I tell Grandpère! I have someone who's on my side. You think I'm alone, but I'm not any more!'

The next day I cried when I told Grandpère what had happened. 'Don't worry,' he told me. 'We'll find you something else, something better, and this time you'll find a good hiding place for it.' True to his word, he came back with an unfamiliar object: a little compass which I thought looked like a big tooth. He said to me, 'You know, this is an invaluable instrument. I'll explain how it works: the blue needle always indicates north. If you place it in front of you, north is there. Now, if you turn round, it still always shows which way north lies. You can turn any way you like and it will always tell you where north is. And that's very important. When you know where north is, you know where south is, you know where east is and you know where west is. With this, you can never get lost. Ever.'

It was fascinating. I played in the farmyard with that tiny compass, which had been set like a jewel into a shell. It was so tiny that you could have worn it on a ring on your finger, but it was perfectly easy to read. I didn't yet know what an important role it was going to play in my life. For the time being, I just amused myself by locating the cardinal points. The barn was to the south, the henhouse was more difficult — south-east, explained Grandpère — and east? I had the feeling that Grandpère was placing a great deal of emphasis on the East. The East was a way of telling me where my parents were. The East was Germany and Poland. He didn't actually know where Maman and Papa were, but Germany and Poland were possibilities. That little needle linked me to them, as if by magic. I could look in that direction and believe that they were out there somewhere, alive. When I went back to '*l'autre*', I had already decided on my hiding place: at night, I'd keep my compass in my mouth, behind my teeth, and during the day I would take it everywhere, concealed in my shoe. No one would be able to steal it from me.

Until then, I continued to play with it on the way back from the farm. Look: the church is to the west. The dog I passed was to the north. It gave me a feeling of power and knowledge. I had a magic secret that no one else possessed: I'd never lose my way. Now I could go where I wanted, when I wanted; the others wouldn't be able to find me — they'd get lost, but I would always know where I was.

Not only was it magical, Grandpère's last gift was also attractive, clasped between the sea teeth of a pretty shell. He couldn't have known that I would really use it. I had no idea yet myself.

Things moved very fast soon after that, a bolt from the blue shattering my fragile peace. I think it was late autumn when Grandpère took me to one side to tell me some very bad news. 'Petit coco, it's too dangerous for you to come here any more. The Boches are in the area and I think it would be better if you stayed at the house for a while, like a good girl. Léopold will come instead of you.'

He hadn't banned me for good, but I understood it differently. I thought he'd already told 'l'autre' to keep me at home, and I knew she wanted to give me to the Germans, and the 'Boches' were in the area. That meant danger. I was Jewish. I'd almost forgotten, and now Grandpère wanted to shut me away like before, when Maman had said,

'Listen, there's nothing we can do about it. We can't go out, we're Jewish. You must understand! But we'll pray that everything will be OK. You must have faith.' And I'd recite the little prayer with her without really understanding it:

Shema Yisrael, Adonai eloheinu,
    Adonai echad.
Barukh shem kevod malkhuto le-olam
    va'ed.

Hear O Israel, the Lord is our God, the
    Lord is one
Blessed be His name, whose glorious
    kingdom is for ever and ever

I couldn't stay shut away with the Virago who hated me — 'If the Germans win, we'll hand her over to them, we'll do ourselves some good.'

Thoughts were buzzing around in my head. For one thing, I wanted to run away, and for another there was the notion that my parents were in the East. The only solution was to find them. I decided to look for them. I didn't think the East looked that far away on Grandpère's map. I had no concept of the distances involved. The East — Germany and Poland — was the green place after Belgium, almost the neighbouring town.

I thought I would just leave Brussels and enter Germany. I was a good walker and I wasn't afraid of anything. Grandpère's geography lessons had been enthralling. There were forests in the East, the Ardennes in Belgium and the Black Forest in Germany. They were full of animals and were bound to be very beautiful. My parents would both be there — I would find them. I didn't think about towns, battles or the war. All I saw was that green country where they were being held after their 'arrest'. Perhaps they were working there, waiting to come and collect me, but I had lost patience. I was fed up with waiting. And I had my compass, so I wouldn't get lost in the forests.

Although I wouldn't have been able to articulate it, I felt as if I were back in the magical childhood realm beneath my parents' bed with my army of animals. The only realities that impinged on me were the immediate threat of being imprisoned at the Virago's house and the dread of being handed over to the *Boches* — perhaps as soon as tomorrow, since they were in the area. I pictured a truck coming to take me away, like the ones I'd seen in the street on the day of the round-up.

And, more than ever, I was haunted by the

image of Maman. I had a desperate need to be with her. Nowhere was safe now that even Grandpère was deserting me. I could say goodbye to the swing he'd made for me under the walnut tree, goodbye to the animals, the hens, the dogs, the sheep and the pigs. I would find others to play with in the forest; they would be my friends. Grandpère was right, you couldn't trust human beings. I was on my own again. I didn't need anyone. All I needed was my legs for walking and a few provisions. My compass and my determination to see Maman would guide me. I was strong, I had sturdy legs, I was tough and I was daring. I wasn't the sort of child to grizzle over a mere scratch. I knew how to do without for a long time. Years later, my husband was the first of many to ask, 'But what made you decide to set off on an adventure like that, in wartime and barely eight years old? You must have been mad!'

I have only one explanation: it was the only way I could continue my life. I knew nothing about war, about death. My view of things might have been unreal, but it served as a point of departure. I was neither a child nor an adult, but something else, I think, a strange mixture of Grandpère's notions and teachings; and the old man had no idea that I'd absorbed them in such a simplistic form. I had to ensure that no one could find me. I had to disappear in the forest, be on my guard against all types of danger and consequently not speak to anyone, because people couldn't be trusted. But I had faith that my toughness and physical strength, as well as my compass, would enable me to find my parents. It was a fixation, an obsession.

I had a goal and the strength to achieve it. My mind was made up. I began to think it through in my own childish way, trying to decide on the right way to go about it: 'If I leave now, she'll come after me or send someone to catch me, so I mustn't leave during the day but at night when everyone is asleep. But if I leave, I must have something to eat, so I'll do the same as those children I saw on their way to school, with a loaf of bread strung round their neck on a piece of string. So I'll need a loaf of bread and a knife. I'll also need something to drink, but I can drink from streams. Still, I'll need a small bag to carry other provisions. Apples are easy to carry; so is gingerbread. I haven't any sturdy shoes, so I'll have to wear the ones I have on.'

No longer than two days elapsed between my making my decision and my managing to acquire the things I'd decided I would need. First, I discovered a small haversack hanging in the corridor. It wasn't very large, but it was strong. I knew where to find apples at the last minute, as well as bread, string and a knife — this last in the kitchen drawer. I'd choose one of the knives that the Virago put on the table to cut meat. A thin, pointed knife with a serrated blade. My compass was hidden in my sock.

That evening, I had dinner once more with the mother, son and husband. I did my best to hide my overwhelming excitement. I was good at pretending, Grandpère had taught me. I can even remember asking him if I would become a bad person like 'her' if I lied. He had smiled. According to him, I had a 'good heart'.

I ate as much as I could beforehand. I would have gobbled down twice as much if the Virago had allowed me, but she always gave smaller portions to me than to anyone else. She told me to go to bed, as usual, and I wasn't taking any risks. I did what I was told, without lingering in the corridor to listen to what she said. It was over; whatever happened, I was leaving that night. All I thought about was Maman. I loved her desperately and it had been painful not having her near me. I hadn't said anything. I had stopped crying, but since Grandpère had told me not to come back to the farm, I'd felt even more abandoned than I had at first. I missed my mother fiercely. After many years, I can say with hindsight that I was in a trance-like state as I was getting ready to leave that house. I was obsessed by the idea that I was the only one capable of finding my mother, the only one capable of saving her — even though I had never clearly formulated the idea that she was in danger, probably because I'd been blocking it out. My mother wasn't dead. It was impossible. I remained convinced of that until the day my husband said, 'Think about it. Given your age and the age she would be . . . '

On the night I left, I felt really strong and I didn't think I'd be away for long. But I had lost track of time — permanently; I think I have remained trapped at a certain time in my childhood, although I can't work out exactly when. Despite that, I have an excellent memory, which is largely visual. I can still see myself walking downstairs in my socks, holding my shoes, trying very hard not to make the stairs creak. I see myself opening the kitchen drawer, taking out the knife and hesitating for a second in front of a pair of scissors before deciding they wouldn't be useful. I left them on the table with the blades parted, like a challenge or a threat.

I had the haversack, the apples — I took just two, which shows how naïve I was — the loaf of bread, which I threaded on to string through a hole made with my finger, then knotted this around my neck, the gingerbread and my compass; then I made off into the night.

It was easy at first. I ran to the little path that led to the canal. I was scared, not of the dark, but that someone would catch me. My plan was to cross the bridge as quickly as possible, to get away from 'her' and from all the 'grown-ups' who'd abandoned me. I was used to running. I often ran back to the house with my basket, so that I could spend longer at the farm. Although everyone said I was small for my age, I was all legs.

When I arrived at the embankment, near the bridge, I was still afraid of bumping into someone who would take me back. Back meant the *Boches* for certain. And, unfortunately, although the night was clear enough for me to find my way, that also meant I could be seen.

The bridge had been partially bombed, and after a few steps I came to a hole. The only way across was to balance on what was left of the iron railings, but I could see the water gleaming black underneath, and I was afraid of the emptiness, afraid of losing my footing. It had slipped my mind before I'd run away that Léopold had talked about the bombing of the bridge, that he'd even been to see the site. This was the only bridge I knew and it seemed impossible to find another. I didn't know where there was one, and I would have had to walk along the canal for too long at the risk of being caught. I decided to retrace my steps and hide until first light.

I found a safe place, near the canal, where I could try to get some sleep, but it was impossible. I heard every noise and pricked up my ears at the slightest rustling. It's one thing not to be afraid of the dark, it's quite another to spend your first night out of doors. Finally, staring wide-eyed into the darkness, I managed to locate the source of the noises. Rats. That was rather comforting — I was far more scared of people than of rats. Grandpère always said that rats were intelligent, because they knew where to go to steal the hens' grain. There were many rats around the canal, but I had no intention of harming them, so they wouldn't hurt me. Anyway, I already had an idiosyncratic way of looking at the animal world. A way out had been formed under Maman's bed and had been confirmed at the farm. The animal world was superior to the world of men and much more powerful. Everything was simple when it came to animals. If the dog wanted to play, I played; if he bared his fangs at me, it was because he wanted to be left alone; if he licked my face it was because he was happy. If he rolled around on the ground with his paws in the air, I did the same. The only difference between, for example, a rat and a cat was purely physical. I simply had to watch the behaviour of a rat that passed by not far from me to realise that it was just looking for food and wasn't at all interested in me.

My real concern at that time was being halted by that hole. I dreaded that walk above the water and that dread was hindering my escape. I hadn't known before then that I was scared of emptiness. I would jump from the ladder in the barn, I would swing high and vigorously under the walnut tree, but that enormous bridge on its four pillars, so high above the canal, was another matter. I talked to myself to cheer myself up: 'We will cross that bridge. We must get some sleep to build up our strength. Afterwards, we'll find the Ardennes forest, and once we're hidden in there we'll be safe.'

Since being alone, I had already begun using the pronoun 'we' unconsciously, as a form of protection, a recollection of my mother's saying, 'We'll have a wash and then we'll do this or that . . .' I realised later, in fact, that I've always had her along as invisible company.

I think I must have slept fitfully, but I also spent a great deal of time thinking about what I was going to do once I had crossed the bridge. I knew where I was here, but the other side was somewhere else. It was the world of Grandpère's map, with town names I hoped I'd recognise, either from repeating them with him or from hearing Marthe, who came from Mons, talk about them. She used to talk about Charleroi, Namur and Dinant, to the south of Brussels. She and Grandpère reminisced about places where they'd enjoyed some good meals before the war. I knew that the canal stretched as far as Charleroi, but I wanted to find the Ardennes, the forest that Grandpère had described, with its tall trees, little brooks and wild boars, a world far away from people, a safe haven for me. I had to avoid humans, large and small. I had to flee danger.

I had decided to proceed in stages and, to my mind, dawn was the first. As soon as I could see fairly clearly, I screwed up my courage and walked to the edge of that gaping hole, trying to focus only on my feet. Every time my gaze wandered, the black water below brought me up sharp. I edged forward on lumps of twisted iron, clutching what remained of the metal guardrail. My haversack was getting in the way because the shoulder strap was too long so it was swinging against my legs. I couldn't stop to tie a knot to shorten the strap, so I had to wait until I was standing on solid ground on the other side. Once I was there, though, I was so proud of myself. I felt like a hero. I'd shown how brave I was, a 'good little soldier', as Papa would have said.

I still thought my journey wasn't going to take very long and I dreamed of bringing my parents back to Grandpère's farm, saying, 'You see, I was the one who found them.' He would be proud of me too.

From there, I continued a little haphazardly, first along the road, then some way into the woods. I slept under the pines and began walking again. It was quite easy going along the roads, which were flat and very straight. When I came to Overijse, the first village at the edge of the forest, I must have been walking for about two days and I hadn't got very far from Brussels. I had already devoured almost all my bread in small chunks and a whole apple. I was hungry, so I hoped I'd find something more substantial to eat in Overijse. I thought I looked like a boy, as I was dressed in a small pair of trousers with an elasticated waist which Marthe had made from a kind of flannelette, a grey sweater with splashes of colour which she had knitted and a short jacket with pockets. I had slipped a dress over the trousers when I'd left, but had soon taken it off, as it was hampering my progress. Until then, I hadn't met anyone. At the entrance to the village, people passed by without paying me any attention, but still I headed towards the distant fields in search of a farm. There's always something to eat at a farm and I thought I might also find some shoes there; mine were already hurting despite my ankle socks. The pain was still bearable, but I knew I wouldn't be able to travel very far in them.

I sat on the ground on a towpath near a farm and watched the coming and goings in the fields. After a while, I noticed a woman in front of the farm. She must have seen me, so I cautiously went over to her. It wasn't likely that she would recognise me, since I wasn't from around there and I was dressed like a boy. In any case, if she did I would soon know and could run away, if necessary. If not, I'd ask her for some bread.

'What are you doing there, girl?'

I ran off immediately. I obviously hadn't made the grade as a boy.

I tried again later the same day. I was still hungry and was eking out my last pieces of stale bread by moistening them with saliva. This time the farm was temporarily deserted.

I found a door at the back and stole a piece of cheese and something that looked like a piece of meat. It must have been cured ham. At that time, everything I ate that wasn't a vegetable I called meat.

When I came out, I aroused the interest of a little white dog, who followed me for a while. I presumed he could smell what I'd just stolen. I waited until I'd put enough distance between me and the farm before sharing some with him. He continued to follow me for a while, until the village was a long way behind us; then he sat down as if he didn't want to go any further. I called to him, because I would happily have continued my journey with him, but he placidly turned round and went back.

I don't remember where I managed to come by some shoes, or rather clogs, which were much too big and which I couldn't wear for long. In any case, I no longer had them by the time I reached the outskirts of Dinant. Grandpère knew that town well. He had told me that the Meuse was lined with massive rocks. After Dinant, I knew I would find the Ardennes. I think it was here that I began to wonder whether I had come too far south and whether I should start going east.

First I walked along the river, but it didn't seem to be flowing east and, as I didn't look very presentable, I didn't want to arouse suspicions by coming into contact with too many people. Still, I must have walked across most of the town. I was extremely hungry and was casting around for an idea when I noticed a small crowd of people under the porch of a church. They showed me how to get something to eat. Some of them were holding out their hands to members of the congregation as they came out of church. I had never seen beggars before, but I suspected that's what they were. They were very poor, and there was even a woman with a baby.

As I drew closer, I saw that they were picking up coins, money, which was no help to me or my empty stomach. I didn't feel able to go into a shop and ask for something in exchange for a coin. People walking past didn't seem to think I was strange, but I was still in Belgium and I was still afraid of being caught and taken back to the Virago.

I positioned myself under the porch, not too near the others, and held out my hand like them. Eventually, a woman looked at me and made as if to give me a coin, but I signalled to her by pointing to my mouth that it wasn't money I needed, but something to eat. She understood, because she went into a bakery on the other side of the square and came back with a buttery cake. This I ate immediately, standing in front of her. I don't know if it was made with real butter, during this period of food shortages, but it tasted wonderful.

'You must be hungry. Is it nice?' She didn't get an answer. I had decided not to talk. That woman may have been charitable, but she evidently wasn't unduly worried about a child of my age begging alone. I soon understood that people didn't care about other people's poverty, even when they were children. Children weren't so important in those days. If she had only tried to hold my hand and take me somewhere, I would have been safe. Once I'd swallowed the last mouthful she left, satisfied with her act of kindness.

I stayed for a moment longer, watching a man who was sitting in a little wooden cart. He had lost both his legs and was manoeuvring his wheeled vehicle with his hands. As people seemed to give him more than the others, I followed him when the beggars went their separate ways. He stopped in a very narrow lane in front of what was apparently his home and stood up on his own two feet. He'd found a way of arousing other people's compassion and I wondered, as I continued on my way, what I could do to make people feel sorrier for me. A bandage around my arm ought to do the trick; I made a mental note to remember that for the next time. I could make one with a strip of the torn dress I still had in my haversack. I'd already used it to try to protect my feet, but that hadn't worked. By now the leather of my shoes had stiffened and was rubbing the tops of my feet raw. I had removed the small leather tongues that were chafing, but since I'd done so my shoes no longer fitted properly and I had huge blisters at the back of my heels. It was difficult to walk, and I was in pain, but I was managing to make headway. My parents hadn't saved me from being captured along with them for me to complain about blisters while I was looking for them. I had to put one foot in front of the other. I had to be tough on myself. Deep down, I was punishing myself for something I hadn't done. I thought I was to blame for their disappearance. I had allowed myself to be seen on the balcony, so it was my fault.

Of course, none of it was my fault, but childhood is like that: unhappiness triggers feelings of guilt. That is what has made me what I am, tough on myself, always making myself put one foot in front of the other. I don't allow myself to feel pain. I order my mind not to feel anything at all until I'm in a kind of hypnotic trance and pain no longer exists, having been overpowered by my will.

On my way out of the town, I noticed a child's bicycle leaning against a wall in a steep street lined with houses. I stole it and rode away — but that didn't last long. It was really too small and it felt as if I was making a lot of effort without getting very far. Tired, I abandoned it when I reached the forest.

Under the cover of the trees I continued to walk, despite my blisters, the chafing leather, the cold and the rain. I kept going and when I was overcome by tiredness, I rested in any type of shelter I could find until it had passed. Most of the time I slept by the roadside, particularly when there were trees; occasionally I slept against farm buildings, although not often. I had also learned the advantages of mangers that farmers had erected outdoors for the cattle: I could climb inside, no one could see me and it was warm. I also liked hollow trees. I remember a very big, very dirty hollow tree that had been inhabited before me by some fairly large animal. As I was little, there was just enough room inside for me to curl up into a ball. I spent some time in there.

I fell asleep quite easily because I was very tired and I didn't yet have the stamina that I later acquired, but I was often woken up by my stomach growling. I tried to appease it by swallowing my saliva. Sometimes I chewed pine needles, which gave me the impression that I was filling my stomach, and sometimes I ate leaves, again just to have something to chew.

I managed to break into several farms, where I found bacon, and eggs which I had to swallow whole. I usually wasn't very fond of the runny whites, and much preferred the yolks, but this was no time to be fussy. I'd eat anything to fill my stomach. Bread was good, butter was a feast and a piece of bacon was banquet.

I also stole the oilcloths that people used to spread over kitchen tables. There had been one at Grandpère's house. Marthe would wipe it with a cloth after the meal and it dried very quickly. I found they were good protection against the rain and cold. They were waterproof on one side and had a type of flannelette on the other. There were never any clothes my size hanging in the hallways or kitchens — everything was much too big — and I couldn't venture further inside the houses. I would keep a careful watch, usually counting in my head to work out how long people took to go out into their garden, for example, and come back inside. Most houses had a door leading into the garden; those were the easiest. As soon as I saw the person go out again, I would dash inside through the still open door. I'd steal what I could see, while counting in my head, leaving a good safety margin. If I had counted to five times ten, I allowed myself three times ten, then made my getaway without looking for anything else.

The mistake I made with my first oilcloth was to cut too big a hole for my head, so that water trickled in when it rained. When I found another I went about things differently: I cut a small hole and forced my head through, which meant that it fitted better around the neck.

As the days went by, I perfected my pilfering technique, which was very simple and dictated by hunger. If I was confident that I could get into a farm, I located the kitchen first. There was always something lying around in the kitchen and there was always a larder. Marthe had a larder, like everyone in the country at that time, to protect food from the flies, and it was easy to steal from them. You just opened the small mesh door and took what you wanted. Cheese, cooked meats, whatever was there. Sometimes I even lifted a saucepan lid, dipped my hand in, then ran off with my mouth full.

It was fairly easy to find things to eat in

Belgium and I didn't suffer too badly from hunger pangs. Of course, there were times I'd go hungry for days on end and I'd eat things that no human being would eat if they weren't starving. I ate worms, grass, leaves and berries, some of which made me ill. But then at least I knew which ones to avoid in the future.

Sometimes, in the evening, I saw distant lights in populated areas. I envied those people for being warm and comfortable, but I was too afraid to go anywhere near them. Still, it was tough when I pictured them eating, and I felt like the poorest wretch in the world. Something to eat! I salivated at the thought. Not having enough to eat was far harder to bear than the cold, the rain or the blisters. But I soon took myself in hand. 'We're not going to waste time. First, we'll clamber up here, then sleep over there. We're not going to waste time. We must move on. I want to find Maman.'

That was the most important thing. She was always on my mind, along with Papa. I thought about him less, for the simple reason that he was with her, and I wasn't. I was unhappy, not him. And that desperate unhappiness gave me the strength to go on, almost against my will. I had no other solution. I had to keep forging ahead, to keep moving so as to avoid collapsing on the spot in tears.

I still have that ability in times of hardship, despite my age. The ability not to cry over material problems, even physical pain, and to keep going. If I'm not making headway, I sleep to forget about it. Only the death of an animal can make me cry.

When my feet hurt, I spoke to them. I can clearly see myself saying to them, 'I'm aching all over, but neither of you is going to let me give up. We must go on. We must take another step because Maman is waiting for us, so you'll take one step, and you another. And another. And another.'

I transformed suffering and exhaustion in my own way, like a game. That's the best way I can explain it. I probably had a fever at times, I may even have been delirious, but I don't think so, because I used this 'game' when anything caused me pain and was in danger of putting a halt to my frantic search for my mother.

Years later, when I had twisted my ankle, I spoke to it in the same way: 'You're painful, that's for sure, you're very painful, but you're going to make an effort for me and we'll keep going.' More recently, my hip had the temerity to break without my permission and the doctor asked, 'Is it painful?' 'Yes,' I told

98

him. 'How painful?' 'It's painful,' I said, 'but I don't know how painful, because I don't know how to evaluate pain.'

One of my girlfriends often says, 'If you go to the doctor, you'll really have to make a fuss, otherwise he'll prescribe you more aspirin for a fractured hip!'

This is because the sensation of pain varies according to the person. It's not caused by the injury itself, but by a person's perception of its severity, and everyone has a greater or lesser ability to ignore it. Although I was young, I refused to give in to pain. Instinctively, I didn't want to allow it to take control of my mind. Back at home, if I bumped myself, Maman would be the worried one. If I scraped my knee, I didn't even notice. I know now that everyone has their own pain threshold and that mine is very high. Pain wasn't the one in charge, I was. My legs were swollen, my calves ached, but they were there to carry me. Their duty was to walk. They would not prevent me from finding my mother. Maman would look after me and nurse my injuries. I had to find her. She was the only one who could understand and do something. She was the only one I trusted, the only one who filled my dreams beneath the trees.

In the Ardennes, I came across a wood

cabin, probably a hut used by foresters or hunters — a real stroke of luck. But when I had only trees, I chose them with care. Fir trees were my favourites: the branches were very long and low, beneath them it was soft and, when it rained — which it did frequently in Belgium — they kept me perfectly dry.

I'd discovered the importance of observation in every respect. I watched what people did and used it to my advantage. Whether someone had left their shoes outside the door, what a husband and wife were wearing when they went out together — whether they were dressed for travelling some distance, which might take them a long time, or just for popping out to tend their spuds, if there were spuds. Digging up three spuds was easy, but collecting eggs was riskier, because the hens squawked. But I could do it.

Stealing clogs in a matter of seconds wasn't difficult, but they weighed my feet down. I filled them with old newspaper so they wouldn't fall off, and then I found that my lacerated feet were black with printer's ink, because the colour had leached out of the paper, and also that shreds were sticking to my cuts. That was worse. I washed myself as best I could in a little stream and had to throw away the paper, which I'd been saving carefully.

My filth kept me warm. I didn't give it a thought. In the early days, when I was with my parents, we had running water only at certain times. No one washed regularly. I remember my mother bathing me in a basin, particularly when my hair needed washing; otherwise it was a lick and a promise under the tap. I also had a bath once in a large tub at the farm. It was in the kitchen and Marthe had filled it with water from the kettles she'd heated over the fire. That had been fun.

On my journey east, I needed water only to quench my thirst, and I'd always find a small brook or a trickle of water somewhere. Sometimes I wolfed down the spoils of my thefts too quickly and my empty stomach would suddenly heave. I'd be sick — and that was terribly frustrating, as though I'd gone to all that trouble for nothing. The only advantage was that the stomach ache I'd have afterwards stopped me feeling hungry, which saved me a day's search for food. But the hunger pangs would soon return.

Managing to survive day after day, being free, and mistress of my own fate, gave me a real sense of self-esteem; I regarded adults as fools. 'You're stronger than they are. They need a house and they don't know how to do what you can do. They're not brave — they're afraid of the cold and the dark. You're not.'

I still lived with my cobras, my animal army. I talked to my troops, I talked to the trees just as I talked to my legs, my hands or my arms. I assured them that everything was fine and that we were unbeatable. That's how I managed. I imagined things the way I wanted them. When I'd finished my day, I congratulated myself: 'You've done well. You're a brave little soldier and you've survived another day. Tomorrow, we'll get through another one. We're cold, but we mustn't think about how cold we are. Thinking about being cold makes us feel cold. We're not going to think about that. Everything is going very well.'

I'd make myself a little makeshift bed, then curl into a ball like a cat and rub my arms and legs until tiredness took care of the rest. I'd fall asleep, my feet rolled in my oilcloth or a stolen shawl, inside a hollow tree, in a ditch or on a bed of pine needles. There was always a way to convince myself that I'd found the best possible shelter and applaud myself for surviving another day.

I didn't regard this as loneliness. I'd always been a solitary child. This was a mission.

4

Starvation

I had made a habit of counting to pass the time. I can trace my first memory of this little quirk back to an odd image. I was in some kind of a cellar with Papa and Maman and there was only one small basement window, level with the pavement, through which I could see people's feet as they passed. I was counting the feet. Where was that? I have no idea. Probably the apartment before the one where they were arrested.

My second memory is of that terrible time when I was waiting for Papa on the school steps. I was counting then, too. I think I'd once been told, 'If you're waiting for something, count to make it come.' I was an impatient, rebellious child and when I wanted something, I always had to have it right then and there. I don't remember what it was I'd be wanting, exactly. I have an excellent memory, but memory and remembering are not necessarily the same when it comes to early childhood.

When walking through a forest or across flat, open country, I counted my footsteps, the trees, the stars. I talked to myself in numbers to keep going. Another ten trees and you can stop. Another so many steps and you can rest. I'd reach the top of a hill thinking I would find a village, but when I saw there was nothing below except a magnificent valley and a river, I'd say to myself, 'What shall we do now? If we want to eat, we must press on. OK, we'll walk as far as that river. I'll have a drink there and we'll take stock of the situation.' As a result, I stopped only at nightfall, to find shelter while it was still light.

I've often been asked how I managed to keep going. You keep going first to find something to eat and then because you always believe that, beyond that tree or over that high slope, you'll find a village, or people or a road sign pointing you in the right direction.

In my case, I also kept going because there was nothing left to go back to. In the evening, when I was exhausted, I'd sit there, thinking back over my day's walk before I fell asleep, and I'd say to myself, 'They are out there, somewhere in the East; if I stop now I'll be letting them down. I must keep going tomorrow.' If I came up against a difficulty,

I'd talk to myself, using the customary 'we': 'We're a bit lost and we're not doing very well.'

I had picked up a pair of particularly massive clogs during one of my forays — unfortunately, they were much too big for me. I had been determined to wear them over my own shoes, but that hadn't worked at all. Although I urged my feet to keep going, the clogs were as heavy as stones and I had to abandon them. Resting for a while near a picturesque river with lovely waterfalls, I saw some young wild boars which ran like the wind. I would have stayed there longer, but hunger kept me on the move. The forest became sparser and at times I found myself walking across flat, open country. There I would count the houses in the distance, constantly obsessed with finding food and shoes.

At one point I acquired a piece of raw meat, which was a real treat. Marthe had let me sample some once, although I hadn't known then what type of meat it was and I hadn't cared; I had enjoyed chewing up the small red scrap, like a dog eating from Marthe's hand. The piece of stolen meat gave me the same feeling of contentment. Sometimes I caught myself remembering the taste of food I'd eaten in the past. I hated foul methylene blue which Maman painted on my throat, but I enjoyed the spoonfuls of cod-liver oil, which Maman kept saying would make me stronger. Meat was the tastiest dish, along with sugar. I occasionally managed to find some meat in farm kitchens, such as bacon, fat or cured meat, but sugar was rare. Since the cake I'd been given when I was begging, I hadn't seen any at all. It certainly didn't grow in the fields with the potatoes. Also, the fields were beginning to freeze over and it was becoming increasingly difficult to dig anything up.

I walked along a railway track which looked as if it might be going in my direction. It was impossible to walk in a straight line in the forest on Grandpère's map, which I could see in my mind's eye. I kept coming up against steep hills and streams that had to be crossed.

At dawn, I'd look for the light and turn my compass in that direction. I'd check where 'E' was and start walking again. Sometimes I'd have to shake it because the needle would stick and I wasn't sure it was working properly; but it just needed time to find the right position. I was often afraid that I'd lost it and I'd break out in a cold sweat. I'd think it was in my pocket or my haversack, but then I wouldn't be able to find it. It was so small that it would turn up in a fold of material or tucked behind a piece of food, virtually invisible. When I was crossing rivers I kept it in my mouth.

The weather was getting colder and the morning frosts forced me to find warmer shelter, so I had to venture closer to farms, where I could hide in the hay or in a cowshed. Although the steaming muzzles of the cattle were just as comforting as a hot bath, I preferred the pigsty because there were always leftovers in the pigs' manger. The cold weather made me take risks. Barns could become traps if I overslept, so I'd remove a plank when I took shelter in them so that there'd be a way out whatever happened. I would sleep in a manger packed with straw, on the alert but in the warm.

I even took the risk of walking through a large village; the inhabitants didn't even notice me. Although I was dirty, I wasn't in rags any more. I was wearing my damp little jacket, covered with a shawl that I'd been lugging around with me for some time, and the blue bonnet Marthe had knitted pulled down over my ears. Although I looked like a beggar, I wasn't begging and was of no concern to anyone. I walked decisively, holding myself upright as if heading for a specific destination, but ready to bolt if anyone spoke to me. I was sure I could outrun anyone who came after me. I found a pair of boots in that village, left outside a door. As always, they were too large, but padded with my ankle socks and some strips of fabric, they kept my battered feet dry for ages.

After that, my route didn't take me past many farms or houses. I don't remember where it was that I stole a handful of dried fish, or where I watched some otters playing, or when I discovered a bitter elder-tree root, some tiny sweet chestnuts and some wild apples, or where I nibbled at some water flowers. Over the years, although the images are always sharp, as if they have been imprinted on my memory, the sequence of events has become a little hazy. I tried and failed to catch some fish in a lake. I saw a hare caught in a snare and managed to set it free, although it scratched me angrily. It couldn't have known I wasn't the human responsible for its suffering. Other animals weren't so lucky; they were already dead when I found them. At that time, I wasn't hungry enough to eat carrion, so I continued on my way.

I can still see the long-haired baby mouse I found in a hole in the ground. It had probably been orphaned after its parents were killed by a nightbird. I fed it with seeds I found in the bushes and gave it a drop of water to drink on my fingertip. Then I let it go with some good advice. It had to do as I did and walk alone like a little soldier. That was all it could do.

I was still in Belgium, but not for long. I don't know how many days I spent walking through my homeland, but it can't have been very many, despite my heading too far south for a while. I'd started out in the autumn; winter was rearing its head by the time I found my way blocked by a wide expanse of fast-flowing water: the Rhine.

Much later in life, I tried to reconstruct the first part of my journey on a map of Belgium. The place-names I had noticed on signs during the war were familiar enough for me to be more or less certain of my route. After the damaged bridge over the canal, I must have gone through Watermael-Boitsfort, then Overijse, Gembloux, Jemeppe, and Bois-de-Villers, where I crossed the Meuse. After catching a glimpse of Yvoir, I crossed part of Dinant, then walked along a railway track to find myself near Marche-en-Famenne. I then trekked through the Belgian Ardennes, and came upon a picturesque river where I lingered for a while. That was the river Ourthe.

When I think about that river, I clearly

remember drinking my fill near some glorious waterfalls. I next came to Malmédy, and I can't remember what I did after that but, instead of heading east, I ended up in Montjoie. I must have crossed the Moselle somewhere near Coblence and then reached the broad ribbon of the Rhine.

I had never seen such a wide river. Even from a distance, it looked black and awe-inspiring. I knew I was in Germany. Hidden in a copse, I'd heard men's voices speaking the same language as Papa had spoken when he didn't want me to know what he was saying to Maman. On the other hand, it was a mystery as to when and where I'd crossed over into enemy territory. It must have been several days earlier. The borders were on the map, not beneath my feet, and the paths I'd taken didn't lead directly to official border crossings. Animals don't recognise borders.

From then on, I had the strange feeling of being close to Papa and, at the same time, a sense of renewed danger. The *Boches*. I had arrived. I was in the East, that mythical destination that in my childish mind was linked to my parents. And I no longer knew what to do, other than keep going. So 'we' were going to find a bridge and wait until nightfall.

I followed the river cautiously from a distance, examining it carefully. I hadn't expected to see such a vast expanse of water; that's not the image you get from a thin blue line on a map. Grandpère had told me about the Rhine in fairly simplistic terms, tracing its course on the map with his finger as he did with the local rivers, adding his own inimitable style of commentary: 'A small stretch in Holland, a small stretch in France, with the rest in *Boche* territory — and now they want it all.'

This description hadn't given me the impression that this was an enormous river. The bridge I first noticed seemed too busy to risk crossing, as on the other side of the mist there was probably a town. A German town, which would definitely not be a good place to show my face. I was no longer in Schaarbeek, the suburb to the north of Brussels, and this wasn't the canal flowing towards Charleroi.

I sat on the ground, feeling rather disconcerted at the sight of that black giant in a strange new world. Had I assumed that when I reached my goal I would simply ask someone where my parents were? What should I do now? Find another bridge and cross to the other side.

I walked for ages before I found the next bridge, which was much narrower. It looked deserted, but as a precaution I spent the night in the undergrowth, huddled up in despair. I was cold, but not because of the mist; the chill I felt was brought on by the enemy. I saw the greyish-green uniforms of the *vert-de-gris* everywhere. Grandpère's *Boches*. Papa's clothes pegs when he mustered his little enemy army opposite mine to teach me 'military strategy'. That phrase, although complicated for someone my age, encapsulated a simple concept: that of winning by outwitting your adversary's attempts to surround your forces. Papa and I had each had four regiments and battalions made up of three or four clothes pegs. I had remembered from previous games that you had to break through enemy lines or stay on your guard while insidiously skirting round the enemy in small groups. I had won only once. I had gathered all my troops together and suddenly charged straight at the enemy, deploying all my battalions. Papa had burst out laughing: 'That's bad tactics. You're not obeying the rules of war.' 'Then they should be changed!' I'd protested.

I could no longer disobey the rules of war. Papa had fled Germany with Maman and they'd had to find a safe place for me because we were Jewish. Grandpère had said that I shouldn't come back to the farm because the

Boches were 'in the area'. One day, I'd shouted 'Filthy *Boche*!' on the tram and Marthe had scolded me because I was endangering everyone. Papa had insisted that he'd never wear the Jewish star, even if it was compulsory, and he'd even sworn when he said it and Maman had made a sign to him and said, 'Shhh! Not in front of your daughter!'

They had both been arrested. Because they weren't wearing it? I didn't have one either — and anyway, what was the point of wearing or not wearing a star? I had yet to understand this symbol, since the only place I'd ever seen it was on Maman's candelabra. Grandpère hadn't mentioned the star to me, so he hadn't been endangered by it. Therefore, I reasoned, the *Boches* must have them.

My mind was buzzing with all these thoughts. So many things about this war were a mystery to me. I was completely at sea. If only the adults had explained clearly what was happening, instead of telling me, as the Virago did, 'We don't talk about that.' If only the woman in black had told me how and why she'd come to collect me. If only Grandpère and Marthe had made me aware of the reality of my situation instead of letting me get used to a happiness that would be short-lived and teaching me where the East was. I'm sure I would have run away just the same, but probably not so far. Although . . .

In my despair at the sight of that vast river, I didn't reason things through like that. All I could think of in my confusion was one rule: a young Jewish girl should never go anywhere near the Germans. But I was there, in their midst — surrounded by them. Where could I find a country without Germans? Where could I find the town full of 'arrested' Jews, where my parents were living? Grandpère hadn't told me enough about Germany for me to know where I was going. On the map it was a big country, with many towns. Even if I slipped into one of them and even if the Germans didn't necessarily know I was Jewish, I wouldn't be able to speak to anyone. I remembered only three or four German words, of which the most useful was *Kartofel* ('potato'). If I tried to break through, I'd be captured. I had to follow the other rule: stay quiet and out of sight while skirting round the adversary.

I muddled everything together: scraps of knowledge, things that Grandpère and my father had said. I couldn't make any immediate plans as I'd done previously when I'd made for a certain tree or a certain hill in the distance and then started all over again the next day. Reality now seemed to be staring me in the face: keeping quiet and out of sight, surrounded by Germans, also meant not being able to find my parents.

That reality wasn't to my liking. I didn't want to abandon the illusion of being a young heroine in search of her mother. I had to keep going because I had no other choice. One day there was sure to be a sign that would lead me to her. But for now I had to get away from the town that I guessed was on the other side of the bridge.

My empty stomach protesting, I scampered fearfully like a mouse over the bridge with only a railway line for company. I was hoping to reach the protection of the trees on the other side. I felt safe only among tall trees. There was no comparison between this forest, though, and the one in the Ardennes. Most of the time it was just copses of trees near human dwellings. As I didn't know where to go, I simply followed the railway track. It was more deserted than anywhere else and was bordered with bushes that could provide cover in the event of danger.

I was soon so hungry but so afraid of approaching a house that I made do with gathering a few potatoes in the fields. I also scratched the bark of rotten trees to extract grubs; I was too hungry to be fussy. I was instinctively searching for meat without knowing that the grubs were indeed protein. I also talked to the grubs, saying, 'I'm sorry, but I have to survive. Thank you very much for letting me survive.'

Gradually I learned to spot large gatherings of crows. I'd disturbed some of these birds when I'd found my first animal carcass, so as soon as I saw them circling overhead I knew there was a dead animal waiting to be eaten. I didn't care what it was. I scraped off fragments of flesh with my knife. In this way I not only managed to find a small amount to eat, but also obtained some strips of fur from a decaying rabbit carcass to wrap round my feet, which were burning from the cold. I'd watched Marthe skin a rabbit. She'd hung it from a nail in the barn, bled it, cut the skin below the head and pulled it off virtually in one piece. For me, the task was much more laborious: the animal had decomposed and I found it difficult to scrape away the dead flesh with its foul-smelling stench. It stank of death; it made me feel sick. Working patiently, I salvaged what I could to line the inside of my boots with the furry side uppermost, under the soles of my feet. I was proud of myself. The idea worked well and kept in a little more warmth. I gave thanks to the rabbit, almost as if I were praying: 'You're dead but you've saved me. I won't be cold any more. Thank you.'

I always felt the need to thank the animal that had brought me some relief. If I stole from a human, though, I felt no remorse. In any case, I didn't regard it as stealing. On the contrary, it was humans who had stolen my parents from *me*, and I hated them.

I didn't go anywhere near one of their houses for a very long time. I'd noticed a cabin, which looked deserted. I watched it carefully before giving up the idea of finding something to eat there. I was far more obsessed with the need to eat than with the icy temperatures of the German winter, which didn't affect me as badly. My stomach complained bitterly of hunger, my head was spinning and I could venture into the fields only at daybreak so as to avoid meeting anyone. I felt dreadfully ill. I vomited and had uncontrollable diarrhoea which knotted my stomach and ran down my legs. It was terrible. Stomach cramps, nausea. But I said to myself, 'That's enough from you, legs, feet, hands and stomach! I'm in charge. You may be suffering, but we must keep going because I have to find Maman, so stop making such a fuss.'

Fortunately, I was never short of water. Sometimes it was stagnant but I could often slake my thirst in a tiny trickle of clear water in a meadow. I'd fill my cupped hands with it and suck pebbles like sweets. In Germany, I even ate earth in an attempt to pacify my stomach. I missed bread badly; it had been quite easy to steal in Belgium, and as I was very fond of it, it had been the staple ingredient of my meals. The sight of bread, the dream of eating it, haunted me for many years to come.

When I started to feel dizzy with weakness, I'd stop near a tree, scratch off some bark and chew it. I'd vomit almost immediately but strangely it made me feel a little better for a while. After throwing up I would yell at the earth. It made so many things grow elsewhere, but here I was starving to death. 'Who will feed me? Give me something to eat.' The earth didn't even provide potatoes any more. At best, all I ate was bitter wild berries, roots or the remains of putrid carcasses, the bones of which I'd gnaw.

I talked to myself all the time. I must have been in a state of delirium brought on by starvation and my complete isolation, but I never stopped obsessively pursuing my goal. 'I've come this far. If something happens to me now and I can't keep walking, I won't find Maman and she'll never know what became of me. I can't let that happen.'

So I'd eat some bark, anything, which I'd

bring up a few yards further on, and start walking again. I just kept going. That was all I thought about, the need to keep going, to avoid staying in one place. I didn't think about death. I don't know why it never crossed my mind that I might die. That possibility just didn't occur to me. I didn't think that my parents could be dead either. They may have been dead already — who knows? — but I've always had my doubts.

One day I was greeted by the wonderful sight of a field of potatoes. I hadn't come across one for a long time. I hid on my stomach in some bushes and watched two men chatting in the field. I was too far away to hear what they were saying. Carefully I edged closer. They were actually singing a song in French about freedom. I was mesmerised, not by the familiar sound of the song, but by the potatoes piled at their feet.

> 'Liberté, liberté chérie
> Le printemps refleurira
> Liberté, liberté chérie
> Je dirai tu es à moi'

I was so hungry that I threw caution to the wind. I stood up and walked over to them. I was going to beg or steal — I didn't really know which.

They noticed me very quickly and one of them said something to me in German, which scared me. I didn't know what he wanted, but I wasn't surprised when he immediately switched to French. Papa spoke the two languages equally well and that didn't mean he was German. I didn't know then that French prisoners worked for the Germans and it never occurred to me to question who these men were.

All I saw was one thing. One of them was throwing potatoes to me as you'd throw a dog a bone, shouting, 'Go on, kid! Hurry up or Fat Bertha will catch us!'

I didn't know who Fat Bertha was — the farmer's wife who employed them or the nickname of some important person — and I didn't care. I warily moved closer, ready to bolt if either of them made a move in my direction, and picked up the potatoes, keeping my eye fixed on the man nearest to me.

'What on earth are you doing here? Haven't you got any parents?'

Suddenly I had tears in my eyes. The word 'parents' had stopped me dead in my tracks.

'Hey! You're not Jewish by any chance, are you? What are you looking for?'

The word 'Jewish' affected me just as deeply. I felt as if it were written all over my

120

face. I wept, neither answering nor daring to take my eyes off that man.

'*Petite*, you won't find anyone here. They're all in the East.'

Even further east! I bolted with my potatoes, running so fast that after a time I no longer knew why I was running. Fear? The shock of hearing someone mention my parents?

Without even cleaning the caked earth from the skins, I ate my potatoes, chewing them for a long time so that I didn't vomit. I was too afraid of wasting the precious food I'd needed so badly. For several days, my vision had been blurred and my head had been floating strangely in space. So had my haversack.

I rested for quite a long time afterwards. I didn't walk much further and I made my food last for several days while I thought about the East. I had believed I was already in the East but, thinking back, I remembered that Grandpère's map had extended even further east. To the east of the East was Poland, which I knew nothing about, then Russia, my mother's homeland, the country where people sang and danced, and drank like fish, according to Grandpère. So I had to go to Poland. The Germans were the enemies, not the Poles. Obviously, I didn't know that people in Poland were trapped in a living nightmare.

I knew just one thing: I had to keep going. But although the compass always accurately showed me which way was east, there were no landmarks to guide me towards Poland. At times, I thought to myself, 'We're going round in circles. Everything looks the same here.'

I came across several cowsheds and gorged myself on pig food. I slept between a cow's legs and filled my boots and jacket with straw. I stole whatever clothes I could find and wore them in layers to keep out the cold, abandoning them as soon as I found others. Nothing ever fitted me. I could have used a cloth greatcoat as a tent, but it was too cumbersome. I preferred my old oilcloth. Clogs and shoes never took the place of my stinking boots lined with rabbit fur.

I had an unbelievable stroke of luck one day when I came across some lumps of bacon rind. They were hanging outside a house on a piece of string, in bundles of two or three. I filled my haversack with them. They were very hard to eat. The rind, which was very salty, had to be stripped off with my knife, cut up and chewed for a long time. The fat inside was delicious and brought to mind the butter at Marthe's farm or milk in the big pail that I used to bring back from the cowshed. I could still taste it, warm and creamy, in my mouth. I didn't find any milk in any of the cowsheds. I risked venturing in only at night, and then there was nothing lying around. I would have had to rob a kitchen, as I had in Belgium, but I didn't dare.

I used the fat to tend my chapped hands and feet. The soles of my feet had become as hard as horn, with deep fissures. My toenails had grown oddly. I trimmed them with my teeth, but they tended to curve over like claws. My feet were always painful. In the mornings, when they were numb and blue, I'd rub them with snow until they burned. The severe pain that accompanied this burning sensation did me good and I could start walking again.

At the end of this cold snap, I no longer felt the snow, wind or ice. All I wanted was something to eat. That was the only thing that mattered any more. It was more important than danger, more important than anything. As soon as I found something on the ground, like acorns or rotten fruit, I forced myself to nibble at them gently with my front teeth like a rabbit. Sometimes I can still taste earth in my mouth. It's an indescribable taste, something you don't forget. You have to have eaten it yourself to know what I mean — just as you have to have slept on a heap of branches in the snow to know that in those circumstances you don't really sleep. You fidget, you turn over, you get up, rub yourself down and fall back exhausted on to branches brittle with cold.

Fortunately, as the days passed, my journey east took me back into the forest where the cold was less severe. I saw a few animals, birds flew off as I approached and I felt much safer. As soon as the trees thinned out and open country appeared, I took cover again. Walking along the edge of the woods was very practical. I could see anyone coming and run away. I could also spot remote dwellings and watch any comings and goings. Most of the time, though, I couldn't get close. I think I spent the entire winter dreaming about a hunk of bread without ever finding one.

I owed my survival to nuts, the frozen carcasses of animals, grubs and raw potatoes, as well as moss, tree bark, leaves and unidentified berries, some of which nearly poisoned me. Not to mention sticky, nauseating pig food — but I survived worse.

One day, stumbling along doubled up with stomach cramps, I came upon a clearing surrounded by massive trees, so tall they made me feel dizzy. In the middle was a carpet of small blue flowers. It was so beautiful that I forgot all about my stomach to roll around in them. Some of my memories are so painful that this one is magical by comparison. I wouldn't have been at all surprised if the animals from my fantasy world had suddenly appeared. I shall never forget that natural cathedral filled with light and the vibrant blue of the tiny flowers growing so densely that they were almost interwoven. It never even occurred to me then that they were a sign that spring was on its way. It was just wonderful to roll around in them as I did, purring like a cat and bathing myself in a beauty that had been missing from my life for far too long.

I also came across another sight, which wasn't at all exhilarating. I had heard a dog barking — I was always drawn to dogs, though I hadn't seen many since I'd left Belgium. So I followed the sound of the barking through the late-afternoon mist, and arrived at a barbed-wire fence. The barking sounded quite close and there were definitely several dogs. This seemed strange, so I walked along the bristling fence until I reached a wooden sign covered with some writing, which was hard to decipher. Letter by letter, I spelled out 'VERBOTEN'. I understood, because I could translate this word. Papa had sometimes used 'Verboten' to stop me doing something. 'Don't go near the balcony, Mishke! It's not allowed! *Verboten!*'

So the dogs were off limits here. I didn't stick around. I ran off into the mist without realising that I'd come within inches of what was probably a prison camp, although I'll never know which one, since I didn't even know where I was.

One fine day, though, I discovered that I'd arrived in Poland. It was a fine day because the weather was fresh and clear and because I had ventured out of the woods and heard the bells of a village in the distance. I can still see the spot perfectly in my mind's eye. There were a few rocks, a brook, some pebbles under the water and grass everywhere. I had just washed my face and hands. I was lying on my stomach in the tall grass and I stood up for a time to look at the bell tower and, in particular, a farm down below, which wasn't very far away. I didn't yet know that I was in Poland, but it wasn't long before I found out — to my cost.

This farm differed from the large German buildings; it was smaller and had a thatched roof. Two figures came out, a man and a woman. They started to walk away and I hoped I might be able to find something to eat quite quickly, but the woman turned round and headed back into the house. I waited. She re-emerged, and finally they both started walking in the direction of the bell tower.

I continued to wait, thinking. If they were going to church as Marthe used to do, this was a good time for me. I'd practised this type of pilfering often enough to be familiar with the drill. If the front door was bolted, I'd look for the back door leading out into the vegetable garden. If there wasn't one, which was unusual, I'd examine the windows. In fact, on this day I climbed in through a window that had been left ajar in the spring sunshine. At that moment I believed in Maman's god, whom I'd occasionally berated when I was dying of hunger. These people had provisions. I found cheese, meat and even some bacon, I think, as well as some eggs. I stuffed them all into my haversack in great excitement. When I came out, I walked around the house and discovered some rabbits in a hutch, a type of small, lowish hut covered in wire netting, with a plank roof. I wanted to enjoy the sun. I didn't often see sunshine in the woods and I wanted to relish my plunder in some semblance of comfort. I sat on the roof of the hut with my haversack around my neck and my legs dangling. I began to eat. I felt happy and I needed the rest. Did I shut my eyes while lifting my face to the sun? In any case, I relaxed my customary guard, which is something you should never do.

I suddenly felt someone catch hold of my legs and pull me to the ground. A man was standing over me, shouting in an unfamiliar language. My immediate reaction was to snatch the knife from my haversack and brandish it. Since I'd left Belgium, I'd changed my knife several times and this one was quite sturdy. The man stepped back — he can't have been expecting that type of reaction from a little girl — and I made off at top speed. I could hear him running behind me, as I raced for the small brook. I was intending to jump over it and make good my escape in the woods. I was almost there when an excruciating pain in my back sent me tumbling head first into the brook. The man had thrown a stone at me so hard that I thought I'd been stabbed in the back. I got up all the same and kept on running, because I had to, but I was winded and I almost collapsed at the edge of the woods. I thought he was still behind me and that he was going to pounce — but he wasn't. He was still on the other side of the brook, shaking his fist at me and shouting incomprehensible words in some language that wasn't German. But at least he had stopped chasing me.

I mustered all my strength and made a last dash for the trees. I kept running even further, then crawled, virtually on all fours, until I thought I was out of reach. Finally, I collapsed against a tree, howling in agony. The pain was stabbing through my back and into my stomach. It felt as if I had a knife planted in the small of my back.

This was the first time I'd howled in pain like this. I'd put up with a lot of pain before but this was worse than anything I'd ever experienced. I howled without stopping until I could no longer draw breath. A very long time afterwards, I was told that the stone had damaged a vertebra, and it can still be seen on X-rays.

I don't know how long I stayed at the foot of that tree; I must have fainted. When I came to my senses, I felt as though someone was watching me. I was right. Fortunately, it wasn't a man. I thought at first it was a big dog with long legs and a tapering muzzle. It was thin with magnificent eyes; it stood there motionless, looking at me. I didn't sense any danger. It was just watching me.

I talked to it in the same way that I talked to all the animals I came across. I said softly, 'What are you doing there? Are you on your own as well? Are you hungry too?' I took the lump of meat from my haversack, pulled off a piece and held it out. The dog still didn't move, so I laid the scrap of meat on the ground in front of me. 'There you are. That's yours. You'll have to come and get it, though, because I can't move.'

It was a wolf. I realised that later. But I would have reacted in the same way whether it had been a wolf or a dog. On the one hand, I was in excruciating pain and couldn't stand up, and on the other, I wasn't afraid. Instinctively I was much more like an animal than a human, and it felt as if I'd always lived alongside animals.

The big dog still didn't move and nor did I, but I was sure that the scrap of meat that lay between us would bring us together.

5

My Wolves

The encounter continued. I tried to move, first one leg, then the other. I could still feel a penetrating ache, so I cautiously raised myself to a kneeling position. Suddenly, a shadow slipped past me, snatching the scrap of meat. I'd virtually stopped paying the 'dog' any attention. I felt as if I'd been sliced in half and I was on all fours, cursing that man and crying with pain, despite myself. It took me a long time to stand up, then put one foot in front of the other. I kept talking to myself: 'Heavens above!' — as Grandpère used to exclaim — 'I'm never going to be able to do this. I'm not going to be able to go on. Come on, spine, you have to move. Forget about the pain. Let's go for a nice walk. We must find Maman. Where is that dog? It would be so nice to have some company, someone to sleep with. Let's see if we can make it to that tree.'

So I began walking. 'There you are, spine, I

knew you could do it! Come on! Easy does it. We must keep going.' I couldn't see the animal any more. I called to it and looked around for it, but I was no longer howling with pain and I wondered if it had been attracted by my cries and had now wandered off. I tried howling again once or twice, but it wasn't the same and the animal didn't reappear.

I had to get away from that place as it wasn't safe, but I was making slow progress. I didn't travel very far that day. Although my haversack was full, I'd paid dearly for it. This was new to me. Until then, I'd always avoided being seen and, with the exception of those two men in Germany who'd thrown me a couple of potatoes, no one — that I'd noticed — had spotted me, despite my having paid many a visit to farms, barns, pigsties and henhouses. I couldn't have survived otherwise. I'd thought I was so clever and cunning. I'd developed what I'd thought were reliable powers of observation, too reliable to allow me to be caught. This time I'd come within a hair's breadth of disaster, through overconfidence. I hated that man for ramming the point home.

I heard a howl, which sounded quite close, then noticed that the big dog was walking parallel with me. Its presence was comforting.

It would stay with me and never leave me, and I'd be able to sleep with it. I had been alone for such a long time. Sometimes, at night, when I was thinking about my mother, I'd rub my earlobe to help me fall asleep, but I missed the feeling of comfort I used to derive from burying my nose in her sweet-smelling mane of hair. At the farm, the dogs' coats used to comfort me in much the same way. I still have a passion for animal fur, although I know now that it's a palliative — a way of recalling my mother's hair. At that moment, though, I just wanted the dog to stay with me. I wanted to tame it to be my friend. I felt so miserable. And it was following me, trotting through the under-growth a short distance away, always keeping pace with me. Sometimes I lost sight of it, but I could still hear it. It must have been able to smell the contents of my haversack.

When evening fell, I rested my back gingerly against the thick tree trunk I'd chosen for that purpose. I'd put a fair distance between me and that vile man and I was exhausted. I laid a few scraps of what I had in my haversack, a little cheese and bacon, on the ground near me and closed my eyes. I must have dozed off as I didn't see the dog come over, but by the time I'd reopened my eyes the scraps had disappeared.

The dog was alone, like me, so we could stick together. I looked around to see where it was and noticed it some distance away, standing on thin legs, sideways on, watching me with its head slightly cocked. It was still there the next day, and the next. I carried on walking, forcing my aching back onwards, although slowly as this was the only way to stop pain knifing into the small of my back. The dog kept moving at the same speed.

First, I noticed it wasn't a male; then it began to howl and I began to wonder if it was actually a dog at all. Grandpère's dogs had occasionally howled, their muzzles pointing up at the sky, but this was completely different. This animal howled for longer and made a different noise. That was when I realised it was a wolf.

I'd seen dogs, rabbits, horses, sheep, lions, snakes and elephants, as well as wolves, of course, in the little animal storybooks brought home by my father, which Maman used to read to me, pointing at the pictures. Fortunately she never tried to scare me with any of those pictures. She simply read out the accompanying text without comment. The wolf lives in the woods, the lion lives in the jungle, the eagle flies through the sky, and so on. As far as I recalled, none of those animals did any harm, so none of them was dangerous. I just regarded that wolf as a superior dog. I didn't associate it with the big bad wolf because I'd never heard the story of *Little Red Riding Hood* or anything like it. On the contrary, I'd played my imaginary games in the animal world; they were my friends and travelling companions. Some animals would allow you near, others wouldn't, and in my own way I understood their behaviour. They were afraid of humans, just as I was.

I was still thinking like a six-year-old, clinging to the vision of an animal paradise, but I remain convinced that an animal's reactions are conditioned by human behaviour. If you're aggressive or afraid, the animal will react accordingly. If you're calm and respectful, there's a chance of forging a bond. After two or three days, a bond had been forged between that wolf and me. I tried to make it come nearer by yelping, since that was its language. It gradually edged closer and closer, warily narrowing the distance between us. I was still curling up in a ball to sleep, because this was the only position that eased my back. The wolf had come no nearer for so long that I'd almost stopped hoping for anything else, thinking, 'This must be a stray creature, which has been harmed by humans, like me.' Then, eventually, it came and lay down against my back. The almost immediate warmth felt wonderful; I was so happy. Lovely and warm, I didn't move another muscle.

Since she was a female, I called the wolf Maman Rita after Grandpère's bitch. She followed me, walking nimbly on her beautiful slender legs, and I spoke to her softly, always in a low voice. Taming an animal meant nothing to me; I just wanted her to stay with me. I didn't want to be alone any more. Falling asleep was a pleasure with that warmth along my back. If I was on all fours, she would shove me with her muzzle and I'd roll over on to the ground. She would wash me with her tongue. I had become her pup: we had developed an almost mother — child relationship, which was even better than the companionship I'd initially hoped for. She would bare her teeth at me when she didn't want me to do something. If, for example, I wanted to put my arms around her neck, she'd draw back her lips to reveal her fangs. I'd take my arms away and she'd quieten down. I soon learned my lesson, even though the learning process could be quite alarming. As soon as she was displeased with something I was doing, she would leap at me, growling and push me over. When she had me pinned against the ground, I was always a little scared, but it was the fear of being punished, like a child who is about to be spanked by an adult. (Although, I myself was never spanked.) Everything would happen very quickly. She'd knock me over, push me to the ground and tower over me, straddling me with her legs. Then, instinctively, I'd lie on my back, yelping like a pup to let her know, 'I won't do anything, I won't move!' — and that was the end of it. I let her do as she wanted. I accepted her rebuke. I didn't always understand what I'd done wrong, but her being there, her grey, fragrant fur, made me feel better about everything. I felt as if I were once again falling asleep against my mother's hair.

The pain in my back had eased, but hadn't disappeared completely. One day, Maman Rita suddenly raced off into the bushes, as if she had heard something. As I didn't move, she ran back to me, seized me by the upper part of my clothing and dragged me away without further ado. Branches and brambles scraped my back as we raced along for quite a distance and the pain flared up again. I hadn't realised she was so strong and powerful. A little further on she let me go, gazing at me intently. I felt as if I couldn't breathe, this time from a combination of pain and happiness. She had protected me. I didn't know what from — I hadn't heard anything — but I was now definitely her adoptive pup.

She could have hurt me badly by seizing hold of my collar if my rags and tatters hadn't protected me from her teeth. She could even have bitten me — but that hadn't even occurred to me.

I should have kept on pilfering food but I was so afraid of losing her that I stayed put. I had nothing left, so I started chewing leaves again. I ate everything I came across, whereas she would disappear, presumably to go hunting. In the end, I decided to follow her example. It had become a necessity. On that occasion, I took so many precautions approaching a house that I spent most of a day and night at it. When I arrived back at the place we'd adopted, she was no longer there. I howled to make myself heard, and after a minute I heard her in the distance. I waited for a while, with my meagre provisions, then ate without her. I was too hungry. I had to accustom myself to the idea that she would eat when she wanted and so would I. That was until she came back with a hare or a rabbit, I don't know which, hanging from her jaws and dropped it in front of me. I was amazed: 'Have you brought me some food?'

Her kill was already almost entirely eaten — there were only a few shreds of meat left

— so I scraped off what I could. There wasn't much there, but I felt so happy: she had brought me something to eat. I gnawed the skin like an animal, right under her nose; she was watching me closely. I said to her, 'You've made me so happy. Thank you. You've fed me. You are my mother, aren't you? There's no doubt about it, you're my mother. My Maman Rita.'

It felt so good to say that word, 'Maman'. This animal was a godsend, a gift from my parents. I was so innocent, acting so instinctively, that I was avoiding danger in the most unlikely way. If I'd been afraid, if I'd run away when I had first seen her, she would probably have behaved differently and would have hunted me like prey. She was a young wolf on her own, probably having been driven away from her pack — typical behaviour, I was to learn many years later, when I started studying wolves. It was up to her to form a new family in her turn. I was so naïve that the sudden appearance of the wolf she had chosen as her mate was completely unexpected.

Once I felt sure that she would either follow me or find me easily, I began to venture further afield again. Sometimes she didn't come back and I spent a night or two without her, unable to bury my nose in her fur while I fell asleep. Then when her absences became longer, I thought she'd gone for good. I still waited for her, though, desperately worried and calling to her regularly each time I returned from a raid. There were houses nearby now, where I could steal eggs. I'd take just enough to stave off starvation, because food was no longer as abundant as it had been in that little Polish farm where I'd almost been caught. I remember living more on animal carcasses and roots. My memories of that period are largely characterised by whether Maman Rita was there or not. I stayed in the same area for a long time to make the most of her company, even though there were clear signs of human habitation. When my she-wolf came back from her own hunting expeditions and I could snuggle up against her to fall sleep, I felt dizzy with happiness. I'd found a substitute mother, and she meant the world to me.

One day, she appeared with a large black wolf — who immediately showed his teeth when he saw me. This male didn't have the same watchful air as Maman Rita and he advanced on me menacingly, his fangs bared. I was terrified; I thought I was going to be mauled to death. I instinctively lay on my back, as I did with her. I was half-expecting him to seize me in his jaws and drag me off into the woods, but she growled at him and placed herself between him and me. The large black wolf hesitated. He made as if to advance and I thought, 'He'll eat me if Maman doesn't protect me.' My memory of that scene is not only rather surreal, but also quite magnificent. Maman Rita growled even louder, confronting the male head on, forcing him to give ground inch by inch. With each growl, her muzzle low, she took a couple of steps forwards and he took a couple of steps back.

For some time I froze, waiting for them to decide my fate, but gradually I realised she had won. She finally came over to me and licked me, as if to say to the other wolf, 'This is mine! Get the message?' She stretched out beside me, without taking her eyes from him. Finding it hard to accept defeat, he walked back and forth for some while, perhaps over an hour; I no longer had any sense of time. He finally accepted it, as if thinking, 'If that's how things are, there's no point in making any more fuss.' He more or less lost interest in me and I thought, 'If he starts to give me any trouble again, she'll be there to protect me.'

In the meantime, he kept his distance. She washed me, and nudged me with her muzzle, obviously reminding him that she had a prior claim to me. Then she walked over to him and did the same thing. She nudged him with her muzzle, as if to tease him, nuzzling at his neck, and they started to play as if I no longer existed. The game didn't last long and they went off together, leaving me alone.

Night fell and I was afraid that he'd come back on his own. It was dark and I couldn't make anything out clearly. I didn't know where it would be safe to sleep. I didn't close my eyes until they came back together and lay down near each other. Maman Rita sniffed me noisily and licked my face and neck several times. She nudged me with her muzzle repeatedly to make me lie down on the ground, then rejoined him.

This was how we started to live together, although our threesome was governed by certain rules. If I stood up, Maman Rita would tolerate that stance, as she knew I didn't represent a danger, but the male would immediately spring to his feet, growling, as if I were a threat. And he had fearsome fangs. With him, it was better to stay sitting or lying down; I experienced several moments of heart-stopping fear before she intervened.

The most important thing was to avoid looking him in the eye. He didn't like that, but if I lowered my head, he'd stop growling and leave me alone. It was a sign of submission that he understood and I now did it automatically, because I'd already tried it with her. Although this was an education with a difference, it was not dissimilar to any human upbringing. It was simply more direct. I made up my mind that if either of them growled at me, I would hang my head like a punished child. If I tried to stand up again, simply because I had to for some reason, then he would immediately make for me and I'd drop back on to the ground, whimpering in the same way as I did with her, and he'd stop short in bewilderment. When he began howling himself, it sounded very different from her howl and I thought to myself, 'My howl doesn't sound the same as theirs, but I'm only little so there's nothing odd about that. Each to his own.'

Although it might sound strange, they were happy. They'd play together, then they'd mate. I didn't disturb them. I knew what was going on. I'd seen the dogs on the farm do the same thing — the female, Rita, had given birth to puppies — so it seemed normal. I was filled with admiration for those magnificent animals which I could observe at such close quarters, watching them leap and jump together, playing like lovers. It was like a dance. Those leaps were remarkable; wolves can jump straight into the air on the spot, something a dog can't do. Droplets of the slobber at the corners of their mouths would spray into the air when they leapt, which I found absolutely delightful. I forgot all about the war. The world of humans was no longer my concern. I was watching something beautiful, which obliterated the distress I felt at being the only survivor, and even made me forget my painful back.

Another rule governing our threesome concerned food. When Rita brought back some prey, perhaps a badger — I wouldn't usually be able to tell exactly — the male wouldn't let me anywhere near the feast. If I stretched my hand out towards the meat, those fangs would snap at my fingers. He would eat first, then she would, and I was allowed to have what was left. When I brought back something to eat, such as vegetables stolen from a garden, they weren't interested in my meal. If I'd been fortunate enough to find some meat, I would contrive to divide it into three small piles before they returned and we'd each eat separately.

One day, they went hunting as usual and shortly afterwards I heard a gunshot. Rita quickly came back, looking very agitated. She circled me, stopped to listen, her ears pricked and her nose in the air, then circled me again.

I could see she was anxious. Every now and then, she lifted a paw and froze, listening to the forest. I tried to go to her, but she couldn't stay still. I wondered what had happened and why she had come back alone, without her black wolf.

She licked me and nudged me with her muzzle, but her attention was no longer focused on me. Something else was bothering her. She trotted off again, and it seemed as if she wanted me to follow her, but I couldn't keep up with her for long; she was moving too fast.

I heard another gunshot, which sounded much nearer, then another. Instinctively, I hid in the tall grass. I thought about the Germans, the man who'd chased me. When I heard footsteps approaching, I flattened myself against the ground. I was only a short distance from a path and I saw some boots passing by at eye level. Raising my head, I saw my she-wolf slung over a man's back.

That grey coat could only have been her. At first, I was rooted to the spot with incomprehension; then I was seized with intense rage, stronger than anything I have ever felt since, and a wave of bitter hatred swept over me. I had only one thought: 'I'll follow him and I'll kill him!'

I lay there, flat on my stomach in the grass,

tears streaming down my face. It wrenched my heart to see her slung over that man's back. I'd noticed cart tracks and traps: the men in this area were hunters, and I hadn't been careful enough. I didn't associate 'hunting' with a rifle. I hadn't yet seen death at such close quarters.

I was determined to kill him. He'd just taken my mother away. My mother had been taken away from me for a second time. That magnificent animal had protected me, kept my back warm, fed me. He had just murdered my mother.

I began walking along the path, my eyes misted with tears. I stopped when the path emerged into open country, and kept watch. He hung the corpse on a hook on the outside of a cabin wall, then calmly went inside. He re-emerged with a chair, sat down and began smoking a pipe. He sprawled there, his chair leaning back against the cabin, his big head resting against the wall. He looked very pleased with himself.

I could see a well and a pail attached to a pulley. That was all. I worked my way round to the rear of the cabin in search of something hard, something I could use as a weapon. There was a wood stack, and tools — and then I found some kind of iron bar. It was very hard and very strong. I chose the bar because I wanted to batter that man to death. I was desperate to make him suffer. I wanted to beat him to a pulp.

If there had been a fork, a pick or a spade, I would have taken that. But all I had was that iron bar when I crept around from the rear of the cabin. The man was sitting beside the door at the front and my wolf was hanging on the left-hand side. I know I was crying, but I wasn't making any sound. I was crying tears of rage. I think I was teetering on the brink of madness at that moment, although I was lucid enough to decide where I was going to strike him. The thought that he might chase after me despite being attacked made me decide to strike at his legs.

Muttering to myself, 'I'll break your legs!' I jumped out in front of him and swung the bar against his legs with all my strength. He screamed with pain and I hit him again. He tried to launch himself at me and fell over.

I don't know if I actually broke his legs, but that's what I wanted to do. He began crawling towards his rifle; I pounced on it before he could reach it. I ran over to the well and flung it into the depths; then, seeing the pail suspended at the end of its rope, I dropped both after it. I don't know if I spoke these words or just thought them: 'You're going to die of thirst — there's water here, but you won't be able to get at it. There's no one around to help you.'

He was on the ground. I watched him crawling and groaning and cursing at me because I'd been stronger than him and he was flat on the ground. And I don't know what gave me the strength to do what I did next — except my hatred, which was as powerful as the feeling of strength that suddenly surged through my body.

I lifted the corpse down from the cabin wall and draped it over my shoulders. It was a dead weight; I broke out in a sweat and my legs trembled, but anger had boosted my determination. I managed to stagger as far as the woods. My strength, generated by a combination of deep grief and a thirst for revenge, was almost inhuman. It was as if I was saying to myself, 'This is too much. They've taken everything else and now they've taken my wolf, the only creature who has loved and protected me since I lost my mother.'

At that time, I really believed that mankind was the universal enemy. It was no longer just the Germans, the *Boches*, it was the entire human race. I had made up my mind. Humans are cowardly because they kill with a rifle. They are liars because you cannot believe what they say. Humans welcome you with open arms and then abandon you. On the other hand, animals fight with their teeth, they cannot lie and they don't abandon you.

I scrabbled at the earth, but I couldn't make a hole big enough. I laid her down and slept against her fur for one last time. It was a dreadful night. I could no longer feel her body vibrating against me, breathing; it was awful. I cried my heart out, because this death was too much for me. She had been my life-saver. Everything merged, the earth on my hands, my tears. I covered her over, as if she were lying in a grave, and I found it very hard to leave her. I walked around in circles; I couldn't leave that place.

I realised that she had paced in the same way around me, after the first gunshot. That hunter or another had killed the male and she knew it. I think I stayed there for three days, crying for her, and for him, and for myself. It was impossible to leave her. No words can explain how alone I felt at that time. Alone and so different from other people. I felt like an animal. I had nothing in common with humans. I had been her pup and now I was on my own, because they had murdered my mother.

I can still see that magnificent creature hanging from a hook. Years later, I thought, 'What men do to animals, they're also prepared to do to humans; they hang people in the same way. Man is the despicable predator of the world. He has learned nothing. He is destroying a beautiful world because he's jealous of it. He is destroying animals because he cannot run as fast as they do, because he doesn't have such a keen sense of smell and cannot hear as acutely. He's jealous of the trees, which are tall and lovely. Man is colourless. He is full of vice. How can I be a human being? It's impossible.' I've never been able to cure myself of thoughts like that.

At the time, I wasn't afraid any more. I didn't even waste time wondering whether there was anyone else in the area, or whether I might receive an unexpected visit. I was so blinded by hatred, anger and a craving for vengeance. Then came the grief. I still mourn the death of the only animal I had loved up until then and whom I regarded as a second mother. When I decided to leave, I spoke to her once more: 'I avenged you, Maman Rita. I avenged you, you know. I'll never forget you.'

But that experience made me much stronger, much more determined. Hatred lent me wings and anger spurred me on. I was oblivious of the pain in my back. That anger kept me going for days. I felt as if I could

150

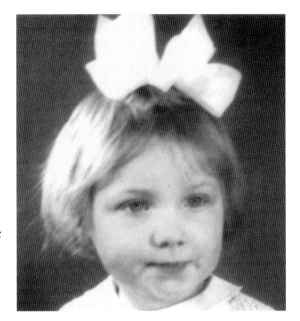

The earliest pictures I have of myself as a child, aged seven. They were taken in the 'Polyphoto' shop in Brussels when I was given my new identity.

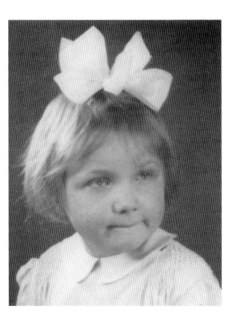

Grandpère
and Marthe
with Ita the
dog.

Marthe and me
with my new doll.

The compass given to me by Grandpère, which I still have.

Starving Jewish children in the Warsaw ghetto.
© *Rex Features*

A pack of wolves playing in the snow in the forest.
© *Powerstock*

At the age of 53 at my Bat Mitzvah with my husband Maurice and son Morris.

Below: This is me in a Russian-style hat I still own, with Gamin who died in 1995. The brim is decorated with brass stars I picked off a dead soldier during the War.

overcome any obstacle in my path. It was an illusion, the only way I could deal with my grief. In truth, the death I wasn't able to mourn properly was probably my mother's. It clothed me in a lasting fury against the human race, their destruction of the natural world and their wars. A part of me had died. The little girl on her journey east had become even more alienated from mankind. I fed on the stomach of a dead horse, I slept beneath wood stacks, I lived in abandoned lairs, gnawed anything, drank rainwater and learned to stay upwind so that no one would know I was there.

As I was walking I came across a railway track which, according to my compass, was heading more or less east. I followed it, always on the lookout, pilfering from fields every so often and keeping my eyes open for crows, which would often indicate the presence of a decaying carcass. I lived on carcasses for a long time. I knew I wouldn't want anything else.

I was covered in cuts and sores, my skin was chapped and my feet didn't look like feet any more. I walked with my toes curled in towards the sole. I had to bite my toenails to stop them cutting into me. I kept walking, not just for the sake of walking but also to survive, like a lone animal. Sometimes I addressed Death. In my nightmares, it took the guise of the woman in black who'd collected me from school. I abused her for taking my wolf-mother and for leaving me alone in the world. I had become a wolf and I was heading east without a great deal of hope in my heart.

6

The Stink of Death

I had moved away from the railway track
— after hearing some voices, I had taken a
path leading as far away from them as
possible. I'd been followed by a dog, which
had been sniffing at me; I must have smelled
of wolf. He'd stopped in front of some bushes
and was nosing around. He wagged his tail,
backed away, then nosed around again. I
thought he might have found an animal
caught in a trap, which could mean a meal, so
I leaned over him and parted the foliage.
What I found was a human body. It was a
man, lying on his stomach, his bare back
terribly mutilated by a star scored into the
skin. Disgusting. The dog was licking him and
nudging his head with his muzzle. I cleared
the branches away and tried to turn him over
on to his back. He was thin, not much bigger
than me. I managed to roll him on to his side
and then I saw another emblem, covered with

dried blood, on his torso, apparently cut with a knife, just as you might carve something on to a tree trunk. This one was a swastika.

I'd come across a number of dead bodies of soldiers since crossing into Poland. They hadn't made any impression on me since the death of my wolf: human beings didn't count. I'd stay just long enough to see whether they owned anything useful. Sometimes I took their shoes, but they never fitted and I soon threw them away, knives always came in useful so I amassed several, but I never wanted their clothes — I was revolted by the smell. Sometimes my attention was caught by something shiny — a brass button, a watch or a ring. I'd play with these little treasures in the same way I'd play with pebbles, and I soon lost them.

But this corpse upset me. I didn't dare touch him too much because I was frightened by the blood-encrusted Jewish star and the swastika carved into his skin. Just as I was about to leave, I heard a groan. He was still alive.

He opened his eyes and I jumped back in fright. I was terrified of that living corpse. He looked straight at me, his eyes open wide, huge, and I could see his mouth moving. He said something in a language I didn't know. I gestured that I didn't understand, so he tried again. I think he attempted several languages, none of which I could make out, except the last, which was French, spoken with a strange accent: 'Germans. Not forget. Not forget.'

That's what I thought I heard. It took him a great deal of effort to gasp out these words. He did his best to move his hand to his chest to indicate another injury further up. A bullet wound.

So this was the work of the Germans. I edged closer and took his hand. He squeezed mine as best he could, his fingers gripping mine, and every time I tried to pull away, he pulled my hand towards him, murmuring, 'Marek.' His eyes seemed to beg me not to leave him, as if he still had something important to say. He repeated 'Germans', then 'party', 'truck', 'waiting', 'all killed', and then 'Me, Marek'. And, most importantly, 'Not forget.'

I concluded from this that there had been some kind of party with the Germans and that people had been tortured, taken away in a truck and killed. 'Germans' and 'truck' went together, since the Germans used trucks to transport the people they picked up on raids. The 'party' remained a mystery. What sort of party would end in torture and death?

But Marek wasn't dead, so I stayed. I'd lost the nerve to run away from that butchered torso, those huge eyes. I couldn't make sense of that type of torture. I had seen dead bodies, both soldiers and civilians. This was war and war meant corpses. You couldn't get any closer to them than I did, owing to my habit of walking along the edges of woods and the outskirts of villages, but I knew nothing of torture. 'Not forget . . . ' Perhaps with his poor French what he meant was 'Don't leave me.' But I definitely heard 'Not forget.' He repeated it several times. I wasn't supposed to forget Marek. I stayed with him until he died.

I covered him with leaves, as I had Maman Rita. The same activity: covering up, concealing death. That was all I could do. Again I shouted abuse at Death. I was speaking to Death all the time now. 'Go away! I don't want to meet you on my path! Don't come near me! You stink!'

I still have sudden vivid flashbacks. When I have nightmares, I see Marek, my wolf and others once more, and I have to chase them away by crying out in the night.

I began walking through the woods again, surrounded by trees — birches, I think. I no longer went anywhere near the edge of the woods. I heard noises suggesting there were people nearby, even on the small roads. I saw wheel tracks and ran away just before a convoy of trucks filed by. The Germans were everywhere. Nowhere was safe from them.

When I came out into a clearing, I discovered some bell-flowers like those I'd seen in Belgium: lily of the valley! Maman used to perfume her hair with that scent. I buried my nose in them and breathed in my mother. In the middle of that carpet of flowers there were some ants. I watched them, saying to myself, 'If I stamp on them, I'll kill them. I have the power of life and death over them . . . ' Then I turned to look up at the sky: 'And so do you, my mother's god, you do exactly the same! You kill without caring whether it's for good or ill!'

What I found fascinating about those tiny creatures was that they were going about their business without knowing that I could kill them, just as human beings were killed, everywhere, completely at random. And I thought, 'I'm lucky. I've been avoiding death.'

How long did that fascination last? I have no idea. Time is an unknown. I have a sense of space, the roads, forests, plains, hills and rivers, but not of time passing. Remembering my childhood is an effort for the old lady I have become. They say that when we grow old we forget the present more easily than the past. I haven't forgotten anything about the past, nor have I forgotten anything about the present, but my past is made up of such distressing fragments that I often recall them in an order in an order which reflects the grief they caused and not chronologically. My memory has recorded precise images of certain places, the words spoken by certain people. I can even recall certain trees that I loved, in the same way as you might love relations. I kissed and hugged certain massive trunks, in front of which I'd prayed and asked for protection. I knew those trees well. They are in my family album along with the wolves, insects and birds.

In one tiny clearing I was surprised to find some cold ashes, the traces of a wood fire. I don't know when I came across that fire but I can see myself standing thoughtfully beside that sign of human presence in a forest so dense I'd believed I was alone. I thought it might have been made by a hunter, some killer or other, so I left the clearing without further ado, even though it looked quite welcoming, and went in search of shelter further off.

The man who suddenly loomed in front of me, threatening me with a fork, had come from nowhere. I spun round — but two more men were barring my way. They were all tall, bearded and armed. My knife was useless against them. The path was too narrow for me to elude them and I'd have been caught in a matter of seconds if I'd tried to make my escape through the thorny bushes. I was surrounded. One of the men addressed me sharply, I guessed in Polish. He obviously wasn't German, but I was still in danger. I shook my head to show that I didn't understand, without saying a word. He persisted; I shook my head again. Then the man with the fork seized me by the collar and forcibly dragged me through the wood to another clearing, some distance from the path, where I saw there was a log cabin completely covered with branches.

In front of the cabin, some men were sitting in a circle. They were poorly dressed, with rags wound round their legs and worn shoes. They looked almost as bad as I must have. Nearby sat some women and children, as well as two or three men in an unfamiliar uniform. I was brought before the man who seemed to be their leader; he also questioned me in Polish. He didn't try any other languages, but in any case, I stubbornly refused to speak. I showed my teeth in a sort of inane grin as I had done with the Virago. Let him think I was just a 'Boeotian', a poor defenceless child who understood nothing at all. The others must have told him how they'd captured me. He growled out several sentences, and then I was unceremoniously made to sit on the ground. The men continued to go about their business: some were cleaning their rifles while others were involved in a heated discussion. The women remained sitting, like me, with the children. After a while, I thought no one seemed to be paying me any attention, so I began to shuffle slowly towards the trees on my backside. Then I got up, stooping down a little, to make a dash for it. I immediately heard shouting and the man with the fork pushed me back down on to the ground, grumbling as he did so. He had a beard and was quite terrifying. I didn't move another muscle.

As evening fell, the women lit a fire and placed an enormous cooking pot over it. I gazed at it with an interest that became even keener when, before long, an aroma of cabbage began rising from it. Soup? I hadn't eaten anything hot for such a long time that I was fascinated by that cooking pot. I'd forgotten that soup existed. In my evening reveries I'd thought about meat, bread, cheese, even jam; the actual aroma of real cabbage was even more exquisite. My mouth was watering. The women served the men, then the children, and then one of them beckoned to me. She was holding out an iron bowl like the others.

It was clear, completely tasteless soup, but it was hot and it felt wonderful in my stomach, and I suddenly felt myself weakening — but I immediately warned myself to distrust such a feeling. I wasn't used to the warmth of the fire. I never made one. The hot soup was undermining my resolve, but I had to guard against softening. I had to stay on the alert so that I could run away at the first opportunity. They'd given me something to eat, so they probably didn't mean me any harm, but I didn't want to remain in their company because they had rifles. They made me drink some sort of colourless liquid which burned its way down into my stomach, while the other children swallowed it effortlessly. They laughed at the face I pulled, shouting 'Bimber!' like a war chant. Much later, when I described 'Bimber', I found out that I'd been drinking a notorious home-made vodka, distilled from potatoes. My stomach has never forgotten it. I remember its name and that of the leader, to whom they often called out — 'Yanus' or 'Janus' was how they pronounced it.

I kept watch all night. The children slept with the women, wrapped in blankets, and the men regularly walked in and out of the cabin on guard duty, but I was never left unattended. At dawn, they broke camp and damped down the fire, and everyone followed the leader, walking single file along the path, with me in the middle.

When we reached the top of a high embankment overlooking a muddy road at the edge of the forest, everyone found a hiding place and waited. It seemed to me that it was because of that road — where, I guessed, something was about to happen — that I was being held prisoner by these people. There was no way out. They were obviously at war; I was surprised that they had women and children with them. As far as I was concerned, soldiers were men in uniform, like the Germans. These fighters were Polish, not German, they looked more like farmers and not all of them were carrying rifles. Although I didn't realise it at the time, I was with a band of Polish guerrillas.

The leader gave a signal, we heard the sound of a motor vehicle approaching and, suddenly, he threw something on to the road. There was a violent explosion, and the men hurled themselves at what must have been a German car. Pulled from the vehicle, the driver fell to his knees; the leader shot him in the head. Another man, wearing an officer's uniform, who had been pulled from the car at the same time, was savagely beaten — and worse — by the men before also being shot. I saw the bearded man even drive his fork into the officer's neck and yank it out again, yelling. Everything happened so quickly and violently that I was frozen to the spot with fear. Strangely, the fork attack upset me more than everything else. Then a young boy, barely older than me, did something odd: he turned a man lying on the ground over and held a feather under his nose. The leader shot that man in the back of the neck. They must have been trying to conserve ammunition.

The children were racing around now as if playing a game. In fact, they were sweeping away the tyre tracks, using branches, while the men completely undressed the bodies, sharing out the clothes, boots and weapons. They pushed the corpses and the car into a ditch and threw branches over them, and that was the end of it. The little band, with me in the middle, headed back the way we had come, in the direction of the clearing.

The next day they started afresh. I was exhausted after an almost sleepless night, broken by nightmares and my burning urge to run away. Another trek, as a group; no one was left behind.

This time they allowed a German convoy to go by without so much as stirring. They were waiting for something else. This was another car, bigger than the vehicle they'd blown up the day before, carrying several officers. The men threw grenades and everything went up in flames. There was a ghastly smell and billows of black smoke. A woman led me off with the other children to sweep the road with branches pulled from the bushes, just as they'd done the day before. And, again, the smoking debris disappeared into a ditch and was covered with earth and branches. It was simple, a tried and tested technique. Everyone took part, including the women and children.

I had to stay with them for several days, because I had no idea how to escape. On the one hand, they were feeding me, and on the other, I was terrified by their violence. I was also unsure where to go if I did manage to escape, because there seemed to be a great many Germans in the area. In the end, the decision was made for me. One morning, a whistle sounded, warning them of impending danger. They decamped, taking what they could, and in their hurry to escape they didn't keep me under surveillance. I pretended to run after them, then headed away in another direction, unnoticed. I ran off on my own, putting as much distance as I could between myself and that violence. I ran with death snapping at my heels. I could feel it. It was everywhere in Poland, in the corpses, on the roads. It seemed to me I would be able to escape death only if I were alone, far away from the living, since the living were killing each other.

I have no idea when, during that frantic journey, I found myself looking at some other living corpses. It was hot. I had climbed to the top of a wooded hill to get my bearings from the lie of the land on the other side. I didn't expect to be so close to a busy road. A group of people carrying bundles were stumbling through the dust. There were several carts, and Germans in uniform. I flattened myself on the ground in the undergrowth to examine this unexpected procession. It wasn't very long — about fifty people, perhaps more; I didn't count them.

I was close enough to make out some of the faces. There were old men, women and children, shabbily dressed, many of them staggering, clearly exhausted. Suddenly I noticed the stars on their clothes. They were all wearing stars! They were Jews! I couldn't believe my eyes. Since I'd been making my way east in search of my parents, I hadn't seen any sign of Jews anywhere. My father's furious voice rang again in my ears: '*Don't talk to me about stars . . . ever! They can stick their bl . . .* ' And my mother's voice: '*Don't talk like that in front of Mishke.*'

I wondered where those Jews were headed, walking like that, barely guarded by two or three Germans. If they were taking them somewhere, I had to go with them. My parents might be there. Were bound to be, in fact. I was convinced of it. To my mind, there could only be one place in the East where the Jews were, so my parents must be with them. Grandpère had said as much; so had those two men in Germany. A lucky break, at last. All I had to do was slip in among the other children. That looked as though it would be simple. I was on a small wooded hill sloping down to the road. All I had to do was cautiously slide down on my backside and hide in the ditch running alongside the road. I had to act very quickly so I didn't miss my chance. I'd learned to react in this way from animals, which approached their prey very slowly; the timing of their attack was crucial because they couldn't afford to fail.

I waited until most of them had passed by. I studied the faces carefully: were my parents among them? For a moment, my heart leapt at the sight of a woman, her black hair tied back under a scarf. I thought I'd just seen my mother! It wasn't her, but those people were the first sign of what I'd been hoping to see for such a long time. At last something was going right for me.

I waited until the German soldier walking alongside the last few had passed, then quickly slipped in behind him. No one paid any attention. Those poor people were walking along without looking around at all, like a herd of beasts. They were grey, dirty and smeared with dust. I must have looked just like them, apart from the star. I don't recall exactly what I was wearing, probably rags and tatters pilfered from somewhere. I would have had bare legs, in any case, and a pair of makeshift shorts, probably cut-down trousers, and I remember the haversack hanging from my neck was empty of food. I was hungry as I hadn't dared to venture near any houses for several days, although I'd glimpsed a couple in the distance from the top of that little hill. The heat was blistering and I was dirty and sweaty like the others, but I had placed a great deal of hope in whatever predicament was driving them on. The only thing that worried me was that I didn't have a star. I was afraid someone would ask me what I was doing there. Those poor wretches didn't take any notice, though. God knows where they'd come from and how long they'd been walking like this.

I didn't know anything about the realities of this world at war, the camps and the ghettos. When the war was over, I learned that at that time, when I had been walking along with that small procession of Jews, hope blooming in my heart, the 'final solution' had already been started by the Nazis. We were officially regarded as a subhuman race that had to be destroyed or sterilised, and that dusty road led to the Warsaw ghetto. Utterly unaware, I was dizzy with happiness because, right then, I was thinking, 'My goal is in sight.' It was a logical assumption. I'd arrived in the East and now I'd found some Jews, so I was close to my parents. To be honest, there are times when I have no idea how I kept going. I had only one source of strength, my extraordinary determination to find my mother and to go on believing my parents were still alive. As well as remarkable physical stamina, of course.

We were walking in the heat of the sun, with nothing to drink, dust caked on our faces, but for me, the hope of seeing my mother again was far stronger than any discomfort. What was the worst thing that could happen to me? That some uniformed German would spot that I wasn't wearing that wretched star? I had no idea that that might pose a mortal threat.

The countryside changed; gradually houses began to appear, probably a suburb. A handful of local inhabitants, mainly children, watched us pass by. When we saw a pump at the roadside, we all rushed over to it. Everyone was jostling for a drink and the Germans simply left us to it, looking just as weary as we were feeling. They didn't seem malicious or arrogant, they just seemed to be escorting us. No one appeared to be a prisoner or under duress to follow them. When I think about it now I can see that it was really odd, but at the time I mistook their resignation and their inability to escape for actual consent on their part. There were so few guards and such an absence of violence that I had no inkling as to what I was going to find. I didn't understand until later that the Germans were so sure of themselves and those Jews so petrified that the former had no need for violence and the latter no desire to rebel.

Suddenly, just as we were about to move off, a woman cried out, holding her head. She was bleeding. I noticed some urchins near us who were throwing stones and shouting, 'Zydzi' — meaning 'Jews' — accompanied by a gesture of goodbye. The group started off again, but no one helped the injured woman. People were worn out; some were sitting on the ground — the German soldier had to force them to stand up. Some were dragging their cases along

169

behind them instead of carrying them.

We slowly entered a village or town and I saw a sign saying 'WARSZAWA' in large letters. I think it was blue and white. On the other side of that boundary stood tall houses, built close together, with balconies from where people were watching us as we passed.

I had joined that group when the sun was high; it wasn't until early evening that we arrived at the large gate in the middle of a stone wall. I could see German soldiers and men in blue uniforms. This seemed odd, and I wondered who these people were. The group had come to a halt and the uniformed men were checking something, although from where I was standing I couldn't see what it was. I thought they were checking the star I didn't have, so I wormed my way further up the line, where I could see that each of the Jews was showing a slip of paper.

I quietly retreated until I was almost at the rear, then nonchalantly went to sit at the side of the road, as if I wasn't part of the group at all. I didn't stir from there. I just kept watch. I had to work out what was happening and how I could get through that gate as quickly as possible. Children without stars were milling about, watching the others file past, and I did the same while I thought things through. There was a wall and a big gate, easily wide enough to take a car; I glimpsed cobbles on the other side. There were a great many more people there than where I was sitting. I concluded from this that it was there that the Jews were gathered. The East. I had to get through, but there were armed soldiers and I didn't have the slip of paper that was being examined by those blue uniforms. A long time after the war, I learned that these men were members of the Policja Granatowa.

I walked off a little way and leaned against the wall of a house; a ragged child was playing there, rolling something along with a stick. Eventually, it occurred to me to ask him if it was possible to get into that place. The simplest way to convey this was by sign language, pointing to myself, then pointing at the wall. He looked at me as if I were an idiot. I gestured again, whereupon he used his stick to draw the star on the ground, then sharply ran the flat of his hand across his neck to show me that behind the wall people were being beheaded. There was no missing the contempt in his gesture, but I pointed to my eyes: I wanted to see for myself. He shrugged his shoulders and sniggered, but pointed at a pile of rubbish against the wall and made a show of digging. As I obviously didn't understand, he cleared the rubbish away himself to reveal a hole, just large enough for a child to fit through. I was so accustomed to sneaking into people's houses like this that it didn't seem at all strange.

I didn't particularly distrust the boy at the time, but later I did wonder whether the route he'd shown me into the ghetto hadn't been too simple and if he hadn't been there to denounce people. When I came back, scared stiff, a few hours later, the hole had been blocked up — although I suppose it's possible that I simply couldn't find it again.

For the time being, I had succeeded in doing what I'd set out to do: I'd got through the wall. I emerged at the corner of a street on the other side. It was very crowded. There were skinny, pitiful beggars, both adults and children, lying on the pavement and people walking past, seeming not to notice. I wondered where those people were going. Why were they walking through the streets? Why were they so indifferent? I rounded the corner quickly to look for a hiding place; the first thing I saw was a corpse lying in the gutter. Although he was partly covered with newspapers, I could still see his feet and head, and people were walking by without giving him a second glance. It was both horrible and completely incomprehensible.

I had to find a hiding place because it would soon be night-fall. I had my back against a fairly large carriage entrance, which shifted behind me, so I pushed it ajar; I found myself in almost complete darkness. I could hear noises, children crying — the place was inhabited, even though it stank so badly that I wanted to leave. I'd glimpsed some German uniforms outside, though, so I stayed behind the door, waiting for them to move on before I made my escape. From my vantage point, I then saw something that chilled me to the bone and left me paralysed with fear. A heavily pregnant woman stumbled on a paving stone and fell over, and then, as she was struggling to stand up, a German kicked her back down on to the ground, put his revolver to her head and fired. Everything happened so quickly — the bang and the body collapsing. I was rooted to the spot. Trapped in a nightmare. I closed my eyes and backed away into the darkness, biting my hand to stop myself crying out. When I peered out into the street again, the two Germans were walking away as if nothing untoward had happened.

People were still walking past, giving a wide berth to the woman lying on the ground in a pool of blood. No one looked at her; she was no more a point of interest than the corpse covered with newspapers. There was no doubt about it, I was in the middle of a nightmare. I had arrived in something that was not life, this was not a town, and these were not real people. I was in shock, numb with incomprehension. I was completely terrified. I didn't know what to do behind that door. Why was I here? Why hadn't I stayed in the woods? Why had I left? My head was spinning with such questions, which I kept repeating to myself like a madwoman. I had to get away from this place!

But I didn't dare. I could not make myself go back into the street. So I slept — although you couldn't really call it sleep — under a stairwell. I could hear cries, groans, noises outside in the street. My refuge stank of urine and the heat was suffocating. When I heard the noise of boots, a stampede and people shouting outside, I peered through the half-open door to see whether this was the moment to make my escape. Suddenly the lights went on in the courtyard opposite, and soldiers began running upstairs.

They threw someone out of the window. I stared wide-eyed into the darkness and almost screamed at the sound of the body thudding into the courtyard. Then they came back downstairs, pushing people ahead of them before gunning them down. I saw it with my own eyes. It's not something I can ever forget. It's as if it has been branded on to my memory: the noise of boots, the light, the screams, the falling body, then jostling and gunfire. I was both fascinated and terrified by the noise of the rifles and the sight of all those bodies suddenly collapsing apparently at random. I was watching shadows die.

After that, everything went completely still. Something was squeezing the air out of my chest. I was suffocating. All I could think about was escaping.

In the dead of night, I thought I'd find my way out easily, but I got lost; I couldn't find the hole in the wall that had been my point of entry. I was upset and shaking. I must have lost my head because I felt so trapped in that insane place. I had no other choice but to return to my stairwell and wait for dawn. Waiting was torture. I didn't move a muscle; my head was spinning. Where was the hole? How was I going to escape? I waited for morning when I guessed there would be a few people about, so that I wouldn't be alone and noticeably not wearing a star. I had to walk like the others, avoiding the uniforms and ignoring the corpses on the ground. Not even glancing at the living. I was afraid of everything. I think I felt a fear there that was profound and all-consuming, the fear of being unable to escape, trapped among all those dead people, surrounded by that stench, with so many people who were alive and yet didn't scream, didn't cry and were walking unseeingly, blind to everything around them, while I was choking with fear.

I still go to pieces when I'm walking through a town when there are too many people. I feel as trapped as I did in the ghetto. I start to panic and sometimes I can't control the fear.

I avoided the uniforms. I folded my arms over my bag, so that no one would notice that I wasn't wearing a star. At one time, I sat on the ground near a young beggar, who was obviously very ill. Poor wretch, did he notice me? I have no idea, but I noticed him. His expression was unbearable. I thought that if no one was paying any attention to that child, they weren't going to spare a thought for me, either. In this place, people allowed their children to die! I hated them. I had to get out.

Further on, a group of children about my height looked as if they were playing a game, so I headed towards them. I preferred to blend in with children to avoid attracting attention. They were speaking Polish, or so I thought, but when I drew nearer, they glanced at me and suddenly began speaking French. They probably didn't want to be understood — like my parents when they spoke in Yiddish or German to exclude me from their conversation. I wasn't wearing a star, so they may have been wary of me. One of the bigger children, who was playing with pebbles, said to one of the others — from what I understood — that he was the winner, because he had four pebbles hidden in his fist. Then he counted them out: 'My father and mother have been deported, my sister is dead, my brother was shot — that makes four. And what do I have left? Just me, so I win!'

Even then I thought it was horrible counting deaths with pebbles in that way. It wasn't that little boy's fault. He was just mirroring his everyday experiences. He was making a game out of the events that made up his daily life. It was terrible.

Mingling with crowds of wraith-like figures, I noticed some men gathering corpses and throwing them on to carts. Sometimes a corpse fell off and the man who was walking behind the cart would pile it back on top of the others. That cart gave me an idea. It was bound to be headed for a cemetery. A cemetery would be outside, beyond the town walls. I had seen only one in Belgium, but nevertheless I was sure that this cart would lead me out of the town.

I started walking alongside it. The corpses

came almost level with my nose and I forced myself to stare ahead with the same indifferent expression as the others. A man was pulling the cart in front, helped by a younger boy, with a third walking behind, and me at the side. The crew of workers was forcing its way through the passers-by. I was just one more ragged urchin; no one took any notice of me. We came to a metal gate, where the cart stopped. A guard turned round quickly to look, then signalled it through. He didn't notice me.

All I could see in the cemetery were piles of earth, stones and deep holes. I ran to hide behind a mound of earth, sand and pebbles. I dug a small hollow to provide better cover and waited for the men to leave. The cart trundled to a halt and the three men threw the tangle of bodies into one of the deep holes. The youngest picked up a shovel and covered the corpses, then they left. I stayed in my hiding place as evening fell. I couldn't see many people except for the guard and several figures at the entrance, near the gate.

I thought there might be a way out, just as there had been from the cemetery in Grandpère's village — a low wall which was easy to climb — but the wall enclosing this cemetery was very high. I crawled over to the foot of it and could see nothing but that wretched wall towering above me. By now I was obsessed with the idea of getting out, of escaping. I had to find a way to climb over. I tried and fell back several times because I was too small, the wall was too high and I couldn't get any purchase with my hands and feet. I followed the wall, still on all fours, hoping to find some raised ground which would give me a bit of extra height. As I groped my way around, suddenly I sensed that the land lay differently: it was sloping upwards a little — although not enough. Pulling out my knife, I began to scrape between the stones, attempting to hollow out first one hole, then another, higher up. Then I started to climb, clinging on so that I could hollow out the next one. It was a lengthy job — I kept falling down and having to begin again. So painstaking was this labour that it seemed to take all night. The pointing was a type of very hard cement, which was difficult to dig out. I would put one foot in a hole, try to grip a protruding stone — and then fall back down. I was getting more and more exhausted, but it was as if I was possessed. Finally, by managing to hollow out enough gaps between the stones, I clambered to the top of the wall — only to be met by shards of glass and barbed wire. My hands and knees were already bleeding, but I didn't care. I wanted to escape from that hell on earth more than anything in the world, even if I scraped every bit of skin off my body in the process. Once I'd regained my balance, I saw in the gloom that the drop from the wall was even higher on the other side. Yet I had no choice but to jump; it was my only chance. I thought, 'What the hell!' — and dropped into the emptiness.

I must have knocked myself out when I hit the ground. I don't remember landing, but when I opened my eyes my ankle was hurting, and I felt as if I needed to be violently sick. My head felt odd, heavy. I don't know how long I'd been lying on the ground. When I regained consciousness, I noticed that my knees and legs were gashed, my hands virtually skinned.

I had to move away from that perimeter wall. I stood up and began walking. I was still in the town, but I could see a railway track and a station; then I heard groans coming from a carriage, which made me run away. I didn't want to listen to the sound of death any more. Coming to a river, with stone steps leading down to the water, I threw myself in and, holding on to the side, drank and soaked my body in the still water, cooling my injuries. I kept splashing myself. I wanted to wake myself up, come to my senses, understand everything I'd seen in such a short space of time. I couldn't. I just kept repeating to myself that my parents couldn't be in that hell-hole, that cruel place where no one paid any attention to sick children on the pavement, corpses or a pregnant woman lying in a pool of blood. Those images went beyond my understanding; they were completely unnatural, and I was too petrified even to try to make sense of them. My ankle was swollen and very painful, but fear had the upper hand so I started walking again, persuading myself that I'd been wrong, that this wasn't the East, that my father and mother weren't here and that I had to look elsewhere.

I walked along the river for a long time with little or no idea where I should be heading. It no longer seemed sensible to keep going east, nor could I retrace my steps, so I was walking in no particular direction. I was limping slightly, I was hot and thirsty and I hadn't had anything substantial to eat for several days. I had just spent two days and probably three nights trapped in a nightmare. By the time I reached a village, near a little river, I was completely exhausted. It was a very pretty place, with sand along the riverbank. I stopped to drink, which felt good — particularly as it was very hot — but I had to find something to eat and a place to sleep.

I was sitting there on the sand when a band of girls and boys ran past me in a panic. Hearing gunfire, I didn't think, I just ran with them. Fortunately before going very far, they cleared away some branches in a grove and jumped into a hole, which had clearly been dug in advance. I jumped in with them. Two of them quickly pulled the branches over our heads. The manoeuvre seemed to have been well prepared; there hadn't been too much to clear away.

Inside the hole, it was like a tomb. The children ranged against the walls gazed at each other in silence. The branches allowed a little light to filter through. We waited. I was so exhausted that I dozed off. When I woke, it was dark and one of the boys was climbing out of the hole; I followed close on his heels to see what he was doing. He led me to an old water pump where we both drank our fill — following him had been a good idea. When we returned to the hole, he carefully repositioned a branch in complete silence. It was strange. Those children — a band of about ten, perhaps fewer — were obviously used to hiding. They appeared to be as poor as me. It was just as good to sleep here as anywhere else, and safer than on the road.

I woke again in the midst of a commotion. The branches were no longer sheltering us. I could see the sky and the kids outside, gathering scraps of bread scattered on the ground, squabbling over them.

Like them, I rushed outside. I grabbed two chunks and immediately devoured them. Then I had a sudden thought: 'Someone knows where we are! We're going to be found! That bread is there to lure us out of the hole!' I don't know if I was right, but my instincts were shrieking that this was dangerous. I tried to pull one of the young girls away with me, but she didn't understand, or she didn't want to. My gestures scared her. She snatched her hand away, as if I were annoying her. She wanted to eat. I did, too, and my mouth was still full of bread, but I ran away.

That peaceful little village on the banks of the river must have been Otwock, about twelve miles south of Warsaw. Years later I spoke about that place with a Polish woman who had been born there and had survived. People fleeing Warsaw had taken refuge there, but unfortunately there had been no refuge outside the confines of the forest, and Otwock had also been raided. I'm still convinced that those children were massacred. I spent a single night with them while they were still alive and took advantage of their bread. I still had what they'd lost by living together — my animal instinct. Of course, those children were in their own country; their parents may still have been alive. If my parents had been there, I would also have stayed. As it happened, though, being a loner was the best protection I could have had. I was used to being free, and all I thought about was survival and finding my mother.

7

The Pack

I was carefully avoiding anywhere inhabited, like villages. I was on the lookout for isolated farms, for water and food that could be obtained easily without my having to take risks. The terror inspired by the ghetto, the corpses in that oppressive heat and that ghastly cemetery had made me long for a forest but, for some time, my route had taken me only through farmland. Whenever I saw people working in the fields, I tried to find out where I was. I no longer had a precise plan.

One day, I came to a field where two farmhands were piling up beetroots. I crawled over to a ditch and listened. They were speaking French, as many people also did in Belgium and as the kids had done in Warsaw — which was still too close for my liking. I could hear snatches of conversation. They must have been discussing work camps or prison camps; one sentence caught my attention because it contained the word 'Belgian': 'And there are Belgian and French labourers at Minsk Mazowiecki.'

If I hadn't been so afraid, I would have asked where Minsk Mazowiecki was, but instead I decided to look for it on my own. I wandered round and round in circles for ages without finding it — although it can't have been far, as I realised years later when I was trying to reconstruct my route. I don't know what I would have found there, and it's probably better that I don't.

When finally I reached a cool forest with tall fir trees and oaks and could sleep at the foot of the trees and hug them in my arms, I felt a little calmer. Since Warsaw, my cuts and scabs had become craters oozing blood. I had tried walking barefoot to ease my toes, which had become cramped and curved in cheap leather boots, but this hadn't really worked. The hard skin had cracked and I'd had to wrap my feet in rags, but the rags kept coming loose, so in the end I put my boots back on. It was simpler than carrying them round my neck with my haversack, which was weighed down with knives and potatoes.

When night began to fall, I'd look for somewhere to rest. It was important to find shelter, some form of protection, a place where I could sit with my back against a rock or a big enough tree trunk. The forest seemed to radiate purity and silence, bombarding me with smells and fragrances, and at last I could shrug off the stink of death which still clung to me.

After several weeks had gone by, I was walking one day beside a small stream. I stepped easily over a dead tree and noticed a waterfall a little further away to my left, opposite a hillock formed of large, irregular rocks. This looked like an ideal vantage point for enjoying some peace and quiet with a good view of the surrounding area. I climbed up to see what was behind the mound of rocks, and when I got to the top, I found some wolf pups in a cave.

Still on all fours, I quietly moved closer. There were four very young pups, playing busily. A short distance away, stretched out on an overhanging rock to keep watch, was a she-wolf, who looked very old and sleepy. A Grandmère Rita of sorts. I immediately decided she was a female because she was alone with the pups — sweet little balls of fluff which were leaping about. They looked like cuddly toys, the type of plaything I'd never had.

They ran over to me and started nibbling my hands, circling around me and jumping on my back. Suddenly, the old she-wolf noticed me. She stood up; the pups immediately bolted for the shelter of their den. I had the impression that she had just said to them, 'What trouble have you got yourselves into now?'

My smell didn't seem to represent any danger, or at least it hadn't worried the elderly, slow-moving wolf — who was, I saw, definitely a female. She wandered over to take a look at me. I let her sniff me all over — my head, my hair, my hindquarters. She seemed intrigued, but not aggressive. I think that to her I smelled more like an animal than like a human. I may still have had a strong scent of Rita and Ita about me. She then sat down nearer the pups, keeping me under observation. I didn't stir until the pups came over to me of their own accord, playfully pushing me with their muzzles. The bravest came out first to tug at my trousers and sniff my haversack, which I never took off as it was my only possession. It was still securely strung round my neck, and well fastened. The other pups followed suit. There was some cheese in my haversack — or at least something that resembled cheese: it was hard and dry, yellow and tasteless. It had what I called the taste of hunger. Many edible things tasted like that. I rarely took much pleasure from eating my plunder, apart from horsemeat or eggs. I don't remember where I'd stolen it from, but I know that I had thought it was a lump of butter — and I hadn't come across any butter for a very long time. I'd been breaking the lump into small daily rations for several days, and now the wolves were very interested in it. So I said to them, 'Do you want my haversack? Well, you can't have it, because I need it. We'll share.'

They ate those crumbs with relish, then went on playing, nibbling my ears, my nose, my hands, and leaping over my back. I was enthralled and very happy. This was the way life was supposed to be, in perfect communion with the animal world.

The elderly grandmother, whom I nicknamed Nounou, evidently didn't think I represented a threat. I was playing with them, and I wasn't being aggressive, so she left me alone. I could see that from her expression — because animals do have expressions. They have an attitude, a way of behaving, a gaze which can give away just as much as human facial expressions. They can be friendly or aggressive, wary or worried, even nervous. I know wolves well. Old Nounou was watching our games as if to say, 'That's OK. I'm not worried. You play, I'll keep watch.'

This was obvious from the position she'd

adopted. She was lying there peacefully, her front legs stretched out in front of her. The pups, having eaten all my cheese, were still sniffing at my haversack. They were trying to grab it, because they could smell the cheese; I had to protect it. They played with my shoes, my sleeves and my jacket. I don't know how much time I spent there, not only watching them but becoming immersed in them, absorbing their smell, biting their ears myself. I had missed the smell of wolf since Maman Rita died. It would have been so good to be like those pups — happy, protected and cherished in their forest lair. I had certainly grown since my departure, but really this just meant I was thinner, I had more nightmares and I was more disillusioned. Otherwise, I was still six and I still cherished the impossible dream of becoming an animal, of acquiring an animal's fur, freedom, superiority and strength.

The adult wolves eventually came back. Large animals. A grey male, then another, followed by two females. They gazed at me inquisitively. Four large, motionless wolves, their eyes fixed on me, waiting for something, although I didn't know what. I knew from experience that a male wolf doesn't behave like a female. Males are unpredictable. Ita had bared his teeth at me at first and growled. These males didn't make a sound, perhaps because there was more than one of them and they felt confident as they watched this strange four-legged animal playing with their children.

Then one female behaved exactly as Maman Rita had. Suddenly she began to walk over to me, eyeing me warily. She sniffed my body all over as the elderly she-wolf had, nudging me roughly with her muzzle to make sure my smell was acceptable: safe for her and the pups, and therefore for the others. I could see her teeth and chops up close and hear her powerful breath travelling over my body, but I wasn't afraid.

There was an element of ignorance in the unconditional love I had, and still have, for wolves. If I had been afraid or had wanted to run away, they would have sensed it. They can sense both aggression and fear, and they can sense the urge to flee. If they do, that's what makes them aggressive. Maman Rita hadn't harmed me and I didn't see why another she-wolf would; I was neither aggressive nor afraid.

There were two males behind this female, and another female. When she had finished her inspection, they came over to me, growling, just as Ita had. I immediately rolled over on to my back, uttering little cries, and the grey she-wolf stood over me, her legs wide apart. The two males and the female stayed close to us, seemingly consulting one another as they walked back and forth, as if they were having a discussion. I didn't move, and the acceptance ceremony ran its now familiar course.

Then the grey she-wolf relaxed her attention, because the pups had run over to her; she nuzzled them tenderly with her muzzle, and the others too left me in peace. Following my instincts, I adopted the same positions that had worked so well with Ita and Rita. For a long time, I stayed on my back, my arms and legs in the air, surrounded by those magnificent beasts. I saw their massive teeth above me and their beautiful eyes. What I felt was more like wonder than fear. I wanted them to adopt me, I wanted to be one of them, and I knew how to act and behave. I was well aware that you mustn't rush an animal. Grandpère had been the first to tell me that, when I was trying to catch the hens to cuddle them: 'You must never force animals. They have to come to you. Let them come. They'll come if they want.' I put the simple lessons I'd been taught into practice. I didn't think there was any difference between hens and wolves in this regard. Communication was a matter of patience and respect. 'I'll accept you, if you'll accept me.'

The pups came back and wanted to play with me again, but I had to be less boisterous with them. I watched the adults, gauging their reaction. I had learned that the rules of behaviour are set by the leader; I didn't yet know who was the leader of my new family. It was merely a question of time and observation. Whichever wolf it was, if he required obedience, I would obey.

I decided to stay with them. It was a large family — anyone with a mind to kill, I reasoned, would find it harder with a pack of wolves than with just one or two. This was an illusion, of course; mankind is the most lethal of predators. Still, I felt safe with them. As far as I was concerned, the peasant who had killed Rita was far more dangerous than a wolf. That magnificent animal would have done him no harm.

Gradually, I made myself comfortable in front of the wolf pups' cave. It was deep enough for them and their mother and there would have been room for me too, but I sensed that the mother wouldn't have accepted that. They played on my back and I rolled on the ground with them, letting them do whatever they wanted. My position was sometimes quite uncomfortable, but it was so good to be there that I didn't care. It was an unforgettable, incomparable experience.

The mother brought them something to eat. This was the first time I'd seen a she-wolf regurgitate meat for her pups. It was fascinating: the pups licked her muzzle until they obtained the food she had been saving for them. After a few days, I was starving — I didn't want to leave them, but all I could find to ease my hunger was water from the stream and a few grubs. There was nothing left in my haversack. I had to have something to eat. Seeing the wolf pups so obviously in good health and well nourished, I began to crave what their mother brought up. I had eaten much worse. Worms, rotting carcasses — they had made my stomach heave and given me terrible stomach ache and cramps, but I was still alive. I didn't see why I shouldn't try to feed from her — I was so hungry. I was sporadically tempted to leave, to go off in search of something, but I thought, 'If I leave, will I be able to find them again? And how will they greet me when I come back? For the time being, I'm here and they're not hurting me, but that could change.' If I were to come back and find myself face to face with a male on my own, he might be annoyed at being disturbed. Aware that the happiness I felt at being part of the small pack was very fragile, I didn't want to shatter it.

So I tried to feed from the mother. I crawled on all fours, as the pups did, to sniff at her lips and lick them. At first, she backed away. I uttered little cries as they did, I persisted and, suddenly, she regurgitated in front of me. I fell upon it; it was warm. She was feeding me! I was her pup just like the others. I revelled in both the food and the maternal affection.

My love of animals reached its peak with that pack. I had already long loved dogs, cats and farm animals, but with the wolves that love became admiration. In my eyes they were superior to humans, and I understood much of their language.

The males, who appeared to be young, left me in peace. From time to time they would look at me and brush against me, but, as I continued to be conciliatory, they would then simply walk off, reassured.

I wanted so much to be one of them, to be a wolf, that one day I made a mistake. After watching the mother lift her leg to relieve herself, I too wanted to lift my leg, so I placed my foot against a tree. Suddenly she growled and knocked me over. I was sure she was about to bite me. I tried to understand — why was I being punished? I uttered my little cries and she stopped growling, apparently having decided that I'd learned my lesson. The problem had been that I wasn't permitted to pee as she did. I realised that all the other wolves, except one male, peed squatting down, like bitches, without raising their leg. That was the difference. I watched them for a long time before taking the risk of peeing on the ground in front of them — making sure I did so like a bitch — and then everything was fine. There were evidently two wolves who were allowed to lift their legs, one male and one female. They were the leaders. I wasn't.

The relationship between the mother and the elderly she-wolf, who kept watch when the others went hunting, could be quite rough, with growls and barks which I called their 'rows'. I would think to myself, 'They're having another row.' I wouldn't be able to regard them in the same way now. Humans have stripped me of my innocence by teaching me about fear, and now I'm aware of the danger. Back then, I was so convinced that nothing could harm me while I was with the wolves that I thought those 'rows' were normal. Eventually one day my adoption was confirmed: they *all* went hunting, leaving me to look after the pups. For me this was a source of great pride — I was a member of the pack with my own role to play.

This did mean that my search for my

parents was postponed. My interlude with the wolves gave me the chance to recover. It stopped me going crazy and allowed me to regain an inner peace; it was like a wall blocking out the horrific things I'd seen. I lived by that waterfall, on that rock. I drank from the stream, just as the wolves did: I saw their muzzles reflected in the water next to mine. It was a magical time and I was truly happy. I belonged to a clan, a family, I was no longer alone and, most importantly, I had the time and the leisure to play; I had missed playing enormously.

From my earliest childhood, I had played on my own, with virtually no toys and without the company of other children. Since leaving Brussels in search of my parents, I had played with pebbles, leaves, feathers or other temporary little treasures that I would sometimes keep or else leave where I found them. But now, in that pack, I had playmates who were always ready to leap about, exchange kisses and play pranks. This was such a precious source of happiness that I as good as forgot about everything else. I became so bold with the mother that I would fearlessly push my nose between her jaws to get her to feed me. This was completely instinctive; it didn't occur to me that it might be dangerous. I didn't regard her teeth as a threat. I managed to obtain a little mushy meat on just three occasions — she already had four pups to feed and I was one too many, so I had to resort to my own devices to find food in the vicinity.

Usually, when wolves catch prey they eat their fill on the spot. The crows then gorge on the remains — often the animal has been only half eaten — and the wolves may come back later. One day, hearing crows when I was near the waterfall, I went to take a look.

The birds were tearing pieces off the remains of a deer in fairly good condition. I wanted a piece of meat myself, and I was tugging it off when a male wolf arrived. I had just enough time to remove my hands. He growled at me and kept me at a distance. The others arrived close behind him and I could only watch as they shared the good meat, fighting over it and gorging themselves. I had to wait until they had eaten their fill. There was no question of my slipping my hand in among them. When they were washing themselves after their meal and none of them was paying any attention to me, I managed to tear off a piece of meat that was almost fresh. It was enough for me. I didn't need to eat as much as they did — although, unfortunately, I had to eat at least every two days, while the wolves could go for long periods without eating anything once their stomachs were full. Still, the remains of their prey usually provided me with enough food, so I didn't often have to go looking elsewhere. I didn't always come across an animal they'd killed on the hunt, but as I explored the territory I usually found something — a hare, a bird or a doe, it didn't matter. What was left after a predator had come and gone would fill my stomach enough to last me two or three days.

During my time with the wolves, I didn't think about anything. I revelled in the beauty of my surroundings, our fellowship based on mutual respect and my little wolf brothers, who were getting bigger. As far as I was concerned, this was really living.

I don't know how long it lasted, but I was still with them when the pups had grown much bigger and were beginning to hunt with the others. I had named their mother Beauté. My father often used to say to me, 'Come here, my beauty,' and Maman would sometimes retort, 'Your beauty hasn't been so beautiful today.'

Beauté was my surrogate mother. I had two favourite brothers, Clair de Lune, because he had a white crescent moon on one paw, and Oreille Cassée, who had been bitten or injured when he was small and had a torn ear. I had a stronger rapport with them than with the others, and they had been the first to accept me.

In the end, I left because of Clair de Lune. He had challenged one of the males, probably his father, by attempting to steal a piece of meat from him. There was a savage fight; Clair de Lune received a good hiding. He ran off with his tail between his legs and the large wolf chased after him to make sure he'd understood that he couldn't come back. It was time for him to fend for himself.

This upset me. The cubs' childhood had come to an end. I was very fond of that young wolf with whom I'd played so happily, and so I went in search of him. He was my brother and my playmate; I wanted to make sure he'd be all right. Oreille Cassée followed me. I looked for Clair de Lune for ages with no success until, one day, I heard him howling on a hill — I recognised his voice. I howled back and he came to find me.

I continued my journey in the company of my two wolves. They often wandered off and went their own sweet way, which wasn't mine, but they always found me. Sometimes I waited for them, sometimes they waited for me. They hunted clumsily, catching small prey, and they still played together like two brothers. One day soon they were bound to join a group where a couple of females would accept them as mates. In the meantime, there were just the three of us. I was still happy, but food was now harder to come by, because they generally ate their prey where they caught it, leaving only feathers or skin. In my search for something to eat I'd have to travel a long way, often to villages at the edge of the forest. Everything was different in that area: the houses were smaller, fewer and further apart and much poorer than in Germany. I was somewhere in Russia, probably near Poland, but I didn't know where. Grand-père's knowledge of geography didn't extend much beyond the big capitals.

One day, coming across a bush laden with juicy berries, I sat down to eat them. Although I couldn't see the plain, it wasn't far away. Immersed in picking berries, I was happily nibbling away at them as I filled my haversack. I was so busy filling it that I didn't notice that Clair de Lune and Oreille Cassée had gone. The times when you relax your guard, when you are preoccupied by hunger, can sometimes be fraught with peril. I didn't see the danger coming.

All of a sudden, I heard a shrill woman's voice shouting, 'Nyet! Nyet!' I dived into the bushes and saw, several yards away, a man in a German uniform. He was so close that I would have fallen over him if I'd walked past that bush with its sweet cargo of berries. Softly I crawled along next to the bushes which formed a type of long hedge between the German and me. I knew I wasn't far from the edge of the forest and I had seen there were houses on the plain. Although I hadn't known there were any Germans here. That made the area far more dangerous than I'd thought. With a bank behind me and the bush in front of me, I kneeled between the two to watch.

A young girl was lying on the ground, screaming, and the uniformed man was ripping off her clothes. She tried to defend herself and he slapped her with all his might. I could see her pale arms and legs writhing. The German who'd knocked her to the ground threw himself on top of her, while she howled like an injured animal. A terrible wail, which grew louder and louder and made my blood run cold. I couldn't move. I'd never seen a rape before, of course. I knew about sex only in relation to animals, like dogs and wolves, but I knew exactly what was happening. I had never heard a she-wolf screaming with pain like this during mating.

The man stood up again, his genitals covered in blood. The girl was unconscious. He refastened his trousers and spat on her. Then he took out his revolver and shot her in the head. In cold blood. I had a clear view of his actions, which followed one after the other in a terrible sequence. He readjusted his clothes, spat, took out his weapon and fired. It was as if he'd counted — one, two, three, four.

This wasn't war as I'd seen it waged by the Polish partisans. This was the gratuitous murder of an innocent young girl, carried out like a military drill. That awful scene has replayed over and over again in my worst nightmares. I was rooted to the spot with horror.

At that moment I recoiled — maybe I even gulped with fear, I'm not sure. My back was pressed up against the bank, so I couldn't run away; the soldier, who must have heard a noise, turned round to look in my direction.

I was lying virtually flat on my back, and I was holding one of my knives — a good, strong blade, like a dagger. I quietly stretched out my arm along my leg, the knife against my right thigh, and closed my eyes. I thought to myself, 'I don't want to die. You're not going to get me, you lousy bastard.'

I heard him coming nearer, the leaves crackling under his boots. He was searching through the bushes. I kept my eyes shut and lay there, stiff as a board, to convince him that I was dead. I felt as if I was actually becoming very cold and icy. Then I felt his breath over me and I thought, 'It's now or never!' I sat up suddenly, the blade held out in front of me, and drove it into his stomach with all my strength.

He tried to grab the knife, but I pulled it out and jumped up, my hands covered in blood. I stabbed him again and again, blindly. He was trying to take his gun from his holster, so I stabbed him frenziedly in the face. I drove the blade into his cheeks, his throat, blood spurting over me. I was beside myself. He gave a gasp, his eyes fixed on mine. It was horrible, because I saw death in those eyes: I stared death right in the face before he fell forward. I stabbed him again in the back of the neck and he collapsed. At last he had stopped moving and I could catch my breath.

I was covered with blood from head to toe. I could even taste it. But I was still alive, my teeth clenched with hatred, the knife dripping blood, telling myself, 'If he moves, I'll stab him again.'

Kicking him to make sure he was dead, I noticed that I'd lost a shoe; it had come off somewhere. He didn't move, though, when I kicked him with my bare foot. I touched him again with my hand to make sure. He really was dead.

I cleaned my knife on his tunic, straightened my haversack and wandered off a little to retrieve my shoe; then I went back and took his watch, like some pointless trophy. I didn't really know what I was doing or where I was. I started running round and round in circles all over the place in the woods, like a madwoman. Suddenly I stopped short: 'What have I done? What happened?'

I fell to my knees, my throat tight with pent-up sobs. I was about to burst into tears or howl, when I saw Clair de Lune and Oreille Cassée heading my way. They conscientiously licked my face, as if to comfort me — but I quickly realised what they were doing. To their mind, I'd just killed a prey; I was covered in its blood. They were used to washing each other after tearing a carcass to pieces. I was a wolf, like them.

When I look back at that scene, it seems incredible. I wasn't even ten years old and I didn't feel like myself any more, I had been out of my mind with hatred at the murder I'd witnessed. I just wanted to cry. Now the taste of blood was making me feel sick, even though the wolves liked it. Their reaction, which made me a wolf like them, a wolf who had just made a kill, restored my composure.

I went over to a stream to soak my burning head in the water. I took off my jacket, my haversack, everything I was wearing, and washed it. My hair was plastered down and sticky. The stream clouded over with earth and blood. I cleared the muck away to drink clear water; my wolves drank beside me. I felt powerful, strong, proud of the duty I'd carried out. When my two companions began to howl, I howled with them. I was alive! I, Mishke, was still alive! Once again I saw the soldier collapse and I congratulated myself on giving vent to my hatred: 'That's for the girl, that's for my parents, that's for my hardship and that's for all those deaths.' I was now feeling a triumphant kind of pride. Now that the wolves had seen me make a kill, I had grown in stature in their eyes. I was definitely part of the animal world now.

That's what I was thinking then. The feelings of depression washed over me only later, when night fell. I couldn't forget the *Boche*'s eyes when I'd plunged the knife into his stomach. Those eyes, wide with surprise. He'd made as if to grab the knife and I had shown the presence of mind to pull it out in time, leaving him with his hands covered in blood, and to continue stabbing him. He had wanted to seize hold of his revolver and I had anticipated him.

Where did I find that strength? Hatred? Courage? Terror? Survival instinct? It was him or me. I wouldn't have survived a normal fight or chase. If I hadn't played dead, lying there cold as stone before sitting up and plunging my knife into his stomach, I wouldn't have survived. But seeing death register in your adversary's eyes knowing that you're to blame is very hard to bear. It was a doubly traumatic experience because the thrill of that fight for survival rushed through me like an electrical charge — I heard that bastard breathing, I saw how afraid he was and I exulted in it. The faster his blood flowed, the more I stabbed him. I was life personified, slaughtering the death and humiliation of that poor girl. I was drunk on revenge and I wanted to live. I wanted to stay alive so badly.

I had not had the guts to look at the poor girl. It hadn't even occurred to me. I knew she was dead, and at the time all I could think about was the incredible victory I had won with my knife. I don't know what I did with that knife afterwards. I can see myself wiping it mechanically, I can see myself looking for my shoe, but then it's a blank. I was running about like a madwoman, and I must have dropped it. I had lost many knives falling over or running away. I still collect them — a lot of them. Like shoes, blankets and food. I hoard them, I lay in stocks: it's a way of getting my own back on the pain, cold and hunger. My knives are now kept in safe places, as if a Nazi might suddenly materialise in a corner of my civilised house. When my husband asks me what still scares me so much that I have to stay on the alert after so many years, I tell him, 'Everything.'

By evening, I was still trembling with emotion after the day's insanity. I wanted to find a bolthole, a hideout, any place where I could disappear and take time out to recover. I would've liked to get away from there, penetrate deep into the forest, far from the paths, the plain, the houses, the Germans. Instead, I collapsed on the spot, near the stream. Clair de Lune stayed close to me; his brother left. I fell into a deep sleep. In the morning, Clair de Lune had also gone.

I walked on my own for a very long time, as if in a fog. For several nights I suffered from nightmares. I heard the girl. I saw the man's eyes above me. The girl screamed 'No!' and shrieked in pain and he raped her, spat on her and finished her off. The smell of human male sweat clung to my nostrils. It wasn't like that with my wolves. When the she-wolf didn't want anything to do with the male, she sent him packing. He had to wait until she was ready. This was a filthy human with no respect for anything. A murderous brute.

He deserved death a hundred times over for what he had done. I shouldn't have felt guilty for killing him — so why did I have those nightmares that made me cry out myself? I was only a child; it was probably all too much for me. I had to force myself to enjoy life after that. I would say to myself, 'Look how beautiful that tree is. You must look at beauty. Beauty will comfort you.'

I always tried to find a way to heal myself. After Maman Rita, after being trapped in the ghetto and after that girl's death, I persuaded myself, 'You're alive. You're heading in the right direction. You're going to find Maman. You must keep going.' I talked to the trees as if I were praying to them: 'You see everything. You know everything. You must protect me. I must keep going. My friends are gone. My family's gone.'

As soon as I stopped praying to the trees, I heard again the shriek of a wounded creature ringing in my ears. So I forced myself to gaze at everything beautiful around me in a bid to escape from the memory of it. I think I've spent my life suffering from depression and trying to find some way, however small, to overcome it.

After so many days of walking through a fog, I didn't even stop to think that I was walking through Russia. All I saw were trees and, just as I didn't then, trees don't recognise borders. I know I slept in an oak on three interwoven branches that formed a comfortable resting place, but I saw mainly silver birches. Those beautiful trees represent Russia for me.

The cold weather returned, bringing hard times and hunger. The meadows were deserted; houses were few and far between. Often they were unoccupied and all they offered was uneasy shelter. Houses were traps — I was very reluctant to take refuge in them. I began to gnaw roots and chew leaves again, scratching the bark to obtain some bitter sap or grubs. I also started to talk to my mother's god: 'You don't exist! Give me proof that you exist! Give me something to eat. Make it appear now! Where can I find something to eat? If there's a farm, show me the way to it! Guide my feet! But you do nothing! You don't exist!' Furiously, I spat in the air, 'Why don't you eat earth? Go on, eat it. You'll see what it tastes like. You don't give a damn about us. You're nobody. You don't exist. Oh Maman, why did you believe in that! Why?' This type of outburst often ended in tears.

I continued my journey without any real landmarks. I was trying to walk south to make a wide detour because, although I had to go west again, I didn't want to take the risk of travelling back through Poland, the kingdom of death. It was hard no longer living as a family with my wolves. I felt different, tougher and more confident, yet more vulnerable.

One evening, just before twilight, I saw a solitary old woman, bowed with age, collecting dead wood in a copse. Not far away was a tiny log cabin, which had to be her home. I waited a while, but didn't see anyone else. She was definitely alone.

I usually made a point of not approaching anyone, but I had been so cold and hungry in the past few days that I walked over to her without taking any particular care. The old woman jumped — she hadn't even heard me coming. I had never seen a face so old, so lined and so withered. She found it hard to straighten up, wisps of white hair straggled from her head-scarf, and she blinked her eyes, as if dazzled. She didn't say anything and nor did I. It was an odd encounter. She was so frail that I felt I should help her. I gathered the wood around her, hoping that she might give me something to eat in return. She threw her wood into a canvas sack which she was dragging behind her; I did the same. Once the sack was full, she knotted the corners and headed towards her cabin, pulling her firewood behind her. Stacking the kindling beside the door, she signalled to me to enter, and when I declined, she started to talk. I didn't understand what she was saying, but the language had a music that I recognised, the music of my mother's tongue. The old woman was Russian. I was in the land of *dusha maya*, 'my soul'.

I refused to go inside. I used sign language to explain that I didn't understand, but that I wanted something to eat. She went into the cabin for a minute, then came back with a bowl of warm milk and a piece of hard, black bread. She watched me greedily eat and drink her meagre fare. The warm milk calmed my stomach cramps. She spoke to me again, making signs to invite me inside, but I shook my head. I was afraid of being shut away; I preferred the cold to a door that might keep me prisoner. I curled up behind her woodpile to sleep.

At dawn, with frozen feet, I found another bowl of milk and another piece of bread in front of the cabin door. I ate, drank and bolted. I thought that the old woman wanted to tame me with her pity, but I wasn't going to let anyone catch me like that. I had no confidence in anyone. When a wolf gave me some of its prey, then it was a gift born of kinship. If a human gave me charity, then I was wary. I could steal and pilfer without remorse, but pity frightened me. I was forced to go out of my way to reject help after the Virago's feigned pity.

Everywhere was in the grip of starvation. I looked for food in the villages but, even when they were still inhabited, the kitchens contained only soup and dry biscuits. I saw bombed villages, devastated farms and haggard farmers. I knew nothing about Stalingrad, the German troops dying in the bloodbath at Kursk. The fall of the Nazis began in old Russia. If someone had told me that then, I would have danced in the snow.

I was walking along a deeply rutted road, feeling no great need to hide as I was so famished — and the landscape so barren. I saw an old man chatting to a younger man. On a leash he was holding a dog, which looked as old as he was, and when I ventured a little closer I realised it was in fact a wolf — although he didn't look like one any more. Tied up with a leather harness, he had a mangy coat, scrawny flanks and sightless eyes. When I held out a friendly hand, he bared his teeth, even though I must still have carried the scent of my wolves.

Poor old grey wolf. He thought I was a younger aggressor, because he was weak and in captivity. The old she-wolf had reacted in the same way whenever Beauté was annoying her. I had just filched a piece of bacon rind which I could have shared with him, but having spurned my friendship he didn't want my pity either. I understood.

I set off again. In one village, I was caught out by a bombing raid in broad daylight which took everyone there by surprise too. I was hiding beside a wall, waiting to break into a house, when everything began to explode and go up in flames. I threw myself to the ground in terror. I had seen the outcome of bombing raids elsewhere, like the bridge in Belgium that had been blown to pieces, and since being in Russia I had seen entire villages flattened, but I didn't know how it was possible to destroy so many houses at once. The bombs fell from a rumbling sky shrouded in black smoke. This was nothing like the time when Grandpère yelled as the planes flew overhead. A wall collapsed near me and, panic-stricken, I ran to find shelter elsewhere. People were running everywhere, and all the doors were closed — I knocked and kicked at them without reply. I was crying with fear under that rain of fire and dust. A little dog threw itself on me, just as terrified. It was barking frantically at the planes, the noise and the bombs. I hugged it, trying to comfort it, and picked it up to find somewhere to take refuge. There wasn't anywhere safe. Everything was smashed to pieces; the street was covered with fragments of furniture, stones, wood, all kinds of utensils and dead bodies. What good would it do me to be trapped in a house? Grandpère had said, 'If I have to die, I want to die out in the open.'

I was trembling, but I gritted my teeth and didn't allow myself to be afraid. I'm outside in the open, I'm brave, and I'm not going to die, because I refuse to die. I've had enough of death. I'm sick and tired of a god who does nothing for me. God is a *schmuck*! I'll never be afraid again!

When silence descended again, the dog was still growling. I released it and it bolted. So did I. I fled that village so that I didn't have to walk among corpses and breathe in the stink of death. The village was on fire and in ruins. I would have to look for food elsewhere. I had to keep going, keep walking, keep surviving so that one day I could find my parents. They at least couldn't be dead. It was unthinkable.

8

Childhood's End

I was walking by a fir wood along the ridge of an embankment overlooking a dirt road. I'd been avoiding flat, open country as much as possible, and since the bombing I'd steered clear of villages and roads. I could see a white dome, probably a church, rising above the roofs of a distant village, which was where the road below seemed to be heading.

I heard the sound of a vehicle approaching, so I quickly dived for cover. A greyish-green covered truck was just rounding a bend. I waited for it to drive past, but it turned off on to a dirt track, made a U-turn and parked, with its rear towards me. I was intrigued by this manoeuvre because the truck had stopped just in front of a largish, deep rectangular hole. Perhaps it was going to unload something. A soldier climbed down from the truck and began to unfasten the tarpaulin. Another German, who looked like an officer and was wearing a peaked cap, also climbed down. The soldier pulled back the tarpaulin and I saw children's faces. He lifted each of the children out, one after the other, and lined them up next to the ditch. I was on the other side, just above the road, so I had a perfect view of this peculiar scene. The child nearest to me was clutching some sort of rag doll. I was fascinated by that little girl: she was blonde, like me — and I hadn't seen a doll for ages. I was lying flat on the ground, behind a tree, my face pressed into the grass, waiting to see what those children of varying ages and sizes might be doing there. There wasn't a sound; none of them spoke or moved, and nor did the soldiers. Each of those kids looked more pitiful than the last, but I couldn't tear my eyes away from the floppy rag doll dangling from the little girl's arm, which every so often she hugged to her chest.

They were so calm. It never occurred to me for a second that they were about to be killed. I just wondered why they were standing side by side in a line. Then the officer aimed his handgun at them and fired a bullet into each child's head. I watched their bodies crumple silently after each gunshot with such a feeling of disbelief that if I hadn't heard the sound of the weapon, I would've thought they were toppling over by themselves. Suddenly I threw up, as if my stomach were trying to climb out of my body, but I couldn't tear my eyes away from that inconceivable sight. As the last little girl, the one holding her doll, the one I could see most clearly, collapsed, I was choking with horror and helplessness.

I had wanted to scream, 'Get away! Run for your life!' I'd had to stop myself from crying out. There was nothing I could have done anyway; it would have been impossible to do anything without endangering my own life. It was driving me crazy. I hit my face against the tree again and again until there was bark embedded in my skin. I had to force myself not to erupt with anger. I was scared to death. Even when you're brave, the fear is still there, lurking in your stomach and at the back of your mind. Fear is what makes you throw up.

The soldier took a shovel from the truck and began covering the children with earth. All those children, none of whom had screamed, or wept, or tried to escape, gradually disappeared under the shovelfuls of earth. After the crack of the gunfire, the rhythmic sound of the shovel breaking the silence was even worse. The truck drove off. I lay there, stunned, my face smeared with vomit. I thought, 'What am I doing? Are any of them still alive? I should have killed that man!' But he would have killed me first.

I was furious that I was powerless to do anything. I felt almost cowardly. Those children crumpling to the ground one by one, each of them dispassionately waiting their turn. The thing that had frightened me most was that they hadn't even tried to rebel; they hadn't screamed or tried to run away. I would've at least made the attempt. They must have been weak, drained of strength, maybe ill, but I didn't understand their passivity, nor did I understand how a man could do such a thing, how he could murder children.

I thought, 'The Germans murder everything, not only women and men, but children as well, all the time. They have no respect for life, they spare no one.' The truck had driven away a long time since, but I stayed on. I vomited bile, water; my stomach ached with it. I stared at that ditch, feeling incredulous, guilty, enraged, but I couldn't make myself go over to see whether there were any survivors or dig up those children's bodies. Nothing moved. I was afraid that the truck might return and begin again: the ditch was deep, and they hadn't filled it right up to the top. There was still room.

The village wasn't far away, so I reasoned

that the children must have come from there. The Germans might bring others. I was a child — I tended to forget that, being so much on my own. Suddenly I was forcibly struck by an idea. The children I'd seen killed seemed to be about my size. I suddenly began to wonder if I was really like them, the same size or bigger. I wanted to know whether the Germans killed children of my size, and therefore of my age, as if they were the only ones under threat of death. There had been very young children there and that's what frightened me. I thought, 'If I'm bigger than the smallest children, then I'm definitely in danger.'

I stood with my back against the tree, stuck my knife into the bark above my head and counted how many of my hands I measured. It didn't give me an idea of how big the others were, but still I thought that compared with them I was tall.

For a long time after the war, I couldn't talk about those solemn children without crying. I saw them crumpling again and again in my nightmares and I'd tumble into the hole with them. I couldn't bear looking after children. People sometimes used to say of me, 'She doesn't like kids!' That wasn't true, but sometimes, if a child threw a tantrum about something silly, I again saw those children falling into that ditch and I couldn't bear that child's tears — and yet I couldn't tell him about the war. Likewise, when I met a German man, I immediately saw that other German in my mind, his eyes, all that blood, and I burned again with incurable hatred.

That day marked the end of my instinctive feral childhood. I perceived danger differently. I was just a little girl ripe for slaughter, a Jewish kid who'd thought she could find her parents and save them. An unattainable childish dream which could end in a nightmarish death. This was war, and I was fighting in it. Like the others, I had been brave, I had been afraid, I had scurried along like an invisible little mouse, determined to find my way. However, I didn't know which way to go any more. I think that for me the East stopped there. I hadn't been able to find my mother. It was terrible.

I kept walking simply because I had no choice, because I didn't want to give up. One day, I noticed some birds of prey circling overhead, far above the tall trees. If I went in that direction, I'd find something to eat — but then I also saw something else in the sky: a slender column of smoke. That thin, feathery, grey plume meant a fire and therefore human beings. Cautiously I forged ahead, my stomach empty. I thought I might be lucky enough to pinch something from a hunter. If it looked too dangerous, I'd turn back and put my trust in the birds.

The smoke was rising from a large hut. Nearby, I could see two men, a woman, and a horse tethered to a tree. They weren't wearing uniforms. One of the men was carving a piece of wood with a knife; he didn't look aggressive as he chatted to the others — but still it was too much for me. I was about to back away silently, when a hand swooped down and seized me by the neck. An enormous hand at the end of an enormous arm, which lifted me up as if I were as light as a feather.

I was so scared that I wet myself. I was wearing at least three pairs of trousers, one on top of the other, rolled up and fastened under my arms. They came up almost to my chin. I was also wearing an old greatcoat over my jacket. I may have been covered with cuts and scabs and I must have stunk, but at least I was warm.

I kicked out, thrashing about like the very devil, while that man, a mighty bearded figure, gazed down at me from his full height. He effortlessly carried me over to the others and deposited me in front of them without releasing his grip. I saw that there were people on the other side of the hut, about ten men with rifles, but no recognisable uniforms. They talked among themselves. Their language sounded familiar, Russian perhaps. At least I knew they weren't Germans. As always, though, I kept silent. They took me inside the hut. In a fairly big room with a low ceiling, there was a stove, some firewood, a table, four or five children bigger than me sitting on bunk beds, a few women, and more rifles in a corner. It was nice and warm in there, no one looked nervous or threatening and the man who'd lifted me up by the scruff of the neck, like a hare, was even smiling as he spoke to the only woman I noticed — because she was beautiful. Grandpère would've called her a 'big, beautiful woman'.

The man who'd been carving his wood in front of the hut stared at me inquisitively and I stole glances at him as well, ready to play the idiot and escape as soon as I could. He tried to make me understand something. Eventually, patting his chest, he clearly enunciated, 'Misha.' Then he tapped mine and waited. As I didn't say anything, he did the same to the tall woman, calling her 'Malka', and then started again, pointing to himself once more, saying, 'Misha.'

I used to be called Mishke once upon a time, and I hadn't heard anyone say my original name since I'd lost my parents. In my head, its similarity to Misha sounded comforting, even affectionate, so I tried to smile at that man and he seemed pleased. I wonder today what he thought of the filthy kid who suddenly appeared out of nowhere and didn't speak his language.

It no longer even took an effort of will to remain silent: I'd become dumb as a result of my silent, lonely and savage animal existence. Human beings were also savage at that time, though. Any manner of horrific thing was possible, so who cared where a kid had come from, what she had experienced or where her family was. I can't have been the only piece of human flotsam left high and dry by that terrible war.

Misha said something else, and then, as I still didn't understand him, he addressed himself to Malka. Watching her busy herself, I realised she was about to give me something to eat. If you've never really been starving, it's hard to understand how much a bowl of hot food or even a chunk of black bread can mean. It was some kind of soup, probably cabbage, as there wasn't much else around. I devoured it all and Malka served me some more. It was such a long time since I'd been given food by a woman and such a long time since I'd eaten something hot! I felt as if this was the first soup I had ever eaten.

It wasn't difficult to understand the positive connection between the food and that woman's smile or that man's kindness as he watched me eat. It helped me remember what normal human behaviour was like and made me feel safe.

Malka was young and very pretty. She wore bulky skirts, with a knife slipped through her belt, and boots. She spoke warmly with Misha, resting her hand on his shoulder and smiling at him. She smiled at me too, pointing towards the children to make it clear that I could sleep there with them too.

I remember I felt like crying. Neither of those two, nor the colossus they called Petia, was a bad person. Their faces didn't betray the spite and violence of the Polish partisans. They did have rifles, though, and Misha looked more like a leader than a simple woodsman and hunter, so they were bound to be fighting the Germans as well. They were comfortable in their big cabin in the woods. When night fell, they ate, drank, sang and chatted, and I let myself be lulled by the music of their voices as I had once been by my mother's voice. Since Malka had given me some food, it hadn't even occurred to me to try to escape. I just felt strangely relieved, which made me want to cry. Although Misha was an imposing figure, he was not at all frightening, and they all seemed to get on so well together and be so happy in one another's company that they fascinated me. These were sane, normal people like Marthe and Grandpère.

The children laughed when they looked at me and the women were obviously talking about me. My first real contact with human beings for such a long time was strange and unfamiliar. An hour earlier, I had been prepared to devour the scraps left by the birds of prey and here I was in the warm, with a full stomach, surrounded by what seemed to be one big happy family. Although I could see they were laughing at me, I didn't know why — or what they had in store for me the next day.

Misha closed the door with a big wooden bar, but I didn't feel like a prisoner. I slept with the children on wooden pallets arranged round a warm stove, enjoying a forgotten feeling of peace and a full stomach. My last meal before that nourishing soup had been bits of a dead horse found in a ditch by the side of a field. It had already been well gnawed and stripped virtually clean; there was nothing very substantial left on it. The carcass had been stiff and hard. It had occurred to me that I could sleep in it to shelter from the icy wind scouring the plain, so I'd curled up inside, as if it were a small cave.

Nothing to do with animals frightened me. I regarded the death of an animal as something natural. During my life with the wolves, I had watched them hunt and bring back kills for me. That was quite natural. I love rabbits and hares and I wouldn't have killed them myself, but once they were dead, my survival depended on them.

The next morning, the door was open. I walked up the three steps of packed earth and went over to see the horse, who was very much alive, still without feeling any urge to run away. I just wanted to touch it, stroke it, remember how it felt to touch an animal's coat. Seeing my interest, Misha gave me some straw and showed me how to brush it down. I was in my element with an animal; everything was fine. Then Malka came over, took my hand and led me away. Using a great many gestures, she tried to explain that I had to wash. I didn't want to. I wrapped my arms around my filth and my haversack to shield my body from this all too human interference. I felt relaxed surrounded by these kind people, but I didn't want to take off my rags.

Without paying much attention to my refusal, Malka had already filled a basin near the stove and Misha was watching me, with a grin on his face. I could tell they didn't want to harm me, but I watched that basin being readied with dread, not knowing how to escape this ordeal. Taking off my ragged clothes and washing was tantamount to removing my skin, and would mean obliterating my wolf smell. I liked to think I was some kind of wild animal, with my scabs and cuts, and my chapped and deformed feet, and yet they were presenting me with a lump of coarse soap, some rags to dry myself with and some clean clothes. I suppose that the evening before, when they were drinking and laughing together, they had been saying to one another that I stank much too badly. That must have been true. I had no idea what I looked like.

I continued to refuse, shaking my head; eventually Misha ushered everyone out of the hut, took hold of a wooden chair and placed it conspicuously in front of the door outside. He sat down, indicating to me that he would stay there, and closed the door, leaving me on my own by that basin. I went over to check that he was really there, torn between the urge to escape and the fear of letting him down. I opened the door slightly and he winked at me.

I was tempted by that bath, though, particularly its warmth. I dipped in my hand first, then eventually I undressed and clambered into the basin. I hadn't had a bath in years, not since the bath Marthe had given me at the farm — and that unexpected memory caught me off guard. I'd even forgotten there was such a thing as hot water.

I watched the steam rising around me. It felt wonderful but, despite everything, I kept a close eye on my haversack and its treasures. My knife, my compass, the German watch, a few bones gathered for gnawing, the odd trifle pilfered here and there. That haversack was my passport, my one invaluable asset, my most important — virtually my only — possession since I'd set off for the East. That and my old jacket, whose pockets were stuffed with all the animal fur I could gather. It still contained tufts of wolf fur. I'd roll it up into soft little balls. These things were much more precious to me than gold. Gold would have had no meaning for me. I wouldn't even have known what it looked like. But with all my treasures spread out on the floor I felt stripped bare and ill at ease.

I resigned myself to using that lump of soap — and the water turned black, really black. All kinds of dirt were floating in it. It was disgusting. As I washed away my filth, I began to feel cold, and my cuts started to bleed as the scabs came off. I used the rags to protect them, particularly those on my feet and legs. I picked up my filthy clothes and put them back on, slipping the clean ones over the top. I did this automatically, out of habit: as soon as I found something more or less my size, I would slip it over whatever I was wearing. If the garment I'd found was too big, I'd cut it down, shorten it with my knife, and then put on the strips of fabric — that was how I cobbled together makeshift leggings when it was cold. I fastened them in place with pieces of rag that I'd made into string; the strips kept my feet from rubbing in boots that were too large for me and could also be used to make simple bandages. If the weather was warm, I'd trot around with bare feet, armoured by my own hard skin, which had become so thick that I couldn't feel anything. I'd sometimes cut off a strip with a small penknife and chew it like gum.

Now I was ready, my haversack slung around my neck. Too much of my hide had come off in the basin, but I wanted to please these people. I walked over to the door and opened it. Seeing me dressed like that, Misha burst out laughing, slapping his hands against his thighs. One of the woman laughed as well, so I laughed with them, without knowing why — they didn't even make me change.

The time I spent with them renewed my

desire to be cherished and loved. It was like a truce period in my personal war, my solitary fight for survival, day after day, year after year. I must have been around ten at that time; I already felt a hundred years old.

I was allowed to explore Misha's territory freely, except for another, smaller, hut some distance away, which was kept locked. I don't know what was stored inside. I regularly brushed down the horse; that had become my job. We always had hot meals based on soup and potatoes. The men drank the same spirit as the Poles had drunk and often sang in the evenings before the group turned in for the night. The women slept with the younger children. My place was with another kid on a wooden bench covered with blankets. During the day, I'd spend a lot of time watching Malka. I admired her and did my best to understand a few words: *voda*, water, *kusok khleba*, piece of bread, *sol*, salt, *myod*, honey. However, my favourite pastime was to sit near Misha. He was a tall, strong leader, respected by everyone. He had a fine knife, which I loved. I'd lost many of mine. In my eyes, knives were vital tools with a wide variety of uses. I couldn't survive without a knife. Noticing that I admired his blade, Misha handed it to me. He watched me carefully, and the way I examined it and

231

turned it over in my hands must have taught him something about me. I was someone who knew about knives. When I gave it back to him he made a gesture that clearly meant, 'You obviously know how to use this.'

When he chatted to the other men, I often heard the word 'Koniev' as if he were talking about someone. In actual fact, Ivan Stepanovich Koniev commanded the First Ukrainian Front and liberated Prague in 1945. His name frequently cropped up in their conversations and they spoke about him solemnly.

The days passed. Every time I found myself in a haven of peace or semi-safety, I didn't want to leave. I needed the rest. Then, one morning, I saw that the horse was harnessed to a cart. The men emptied the hut and brought out the rifles, and Misha came over and took my hand. He wanted me to get into the cart with the other children. I didn't want to go.

He seemed annoyed. How could I tell him that I couldn't go with them? I was going my own way because I still hadn't found my parents. I'd started thinking that they might be looking for me back there, in Belgium. I had to cling to something. If I'd accepted that my mother must be dead, I would have stayed where I was and would almost certainly have died as well. Since I'd been safe with Misha and Malka, I'd been missing Maman even more than ever. As soon as I was alone, I would cry over her absence, thumping the ground with my fist. For now, it was impossible to talk about it, tell them everything, so, like a stubborn mule, I shook my head, pointing at an imaginary road behind me.

In any case, they couldn't help me any more. I guessed they were going to fight, that they were taking the women and children with them, because everyone fought here. The women and children were waiting for me, Misha insisted, but I shook my head bravely, despite the sorrow I felt at watching them leave. My desolation at being alone again as well as my determination must have shown in my eyes, for he then gave me the best gift in the world: a knife similar to his, as well as some black bread and a fur hat like the one they all wore. A chapka. I rummaged through my haversack. I wanted to give him something as well. I held out one of my treasures to him, the German watch. He accepted it, then laid his hand on my head enveloped in the new hat, and they left.

Later on, a great deal later, after the Russians had planted their flag on the Reichstadt, I would have liked to have been with them. I had lost my war, lost my parents,

I hadn't won any victories or punished anyone and no one had ever asked my forgiveness.

Back then, I stood in front of that deserted hut, feeling sad but in far better physical condition than before. The winter in the Ukraine was not as harsh as in Germany. I had been fed and kept warm, and I felt fit enough to set off again — heading west this time. My journey west was taking me through Romania and Yugoslavia, though, and I hadn't given a thought to the mountains or ravines that lay in my path.

I set off on a lonely forced march. I would have liked to have been able to run and jump over all the obstacles that lay ahead on my journey back to Belgium, but Grandpère's tiny compass couldn't help me with that.

I'd left the forest behind, because there was no other choice, and I was walking through flat, open country when I came to a scene of carnage. More dead bodies. Russian soldiers. I contemplated them with the indifference that served as my protective shell. I noticed some gold stars on a cap and an epaulette. Taking the four from the cap and three from one shoulder, I added them to the treasures in my haversack. I still have them. I regarded them as proper keepsakes of the war, the one waged by the Russians, by Misha. I was taking away a symbol linked to my mother's Russian origins, intending to give the stars to her as soon as I'd found her.

When I saw a German truck burning in the distance, with Russians dancing around it, I thought it meant victory. 'This time,' I thought, 'I can walk freely. I won't cross the path of any more *Boches*.' Unfortunately, there was apparently still one left, standing on his own in front of a bridge that I absolutely had to cross. I was surrounded by mountains, and that bridge spanned a yawning chasm. I watched that wretched German stationed there, rifle in hand, for quite a time. It was odd that he should have been completely alone. He was keeping watch over the bridge, but there no one was crossing it.

I felt a little as I had at the farm when, after climbing the ladder in the barn for the first time, I didn't know whether or not to jump down into the hay, because Marthe was scared, protesting, 'Come down here! You'll hurt yourself!' At the same time, 'Jump!' urged Grandpère. 'Don't be afraid!' I had jumped and he'd taught me one of his favourite, unforgettable lessons: 'When you have to make a decision, you must make it quickly, otherwise it'll be too late.'

Crossing that bridge was similar. I had to do it straight away. I moved forward, my hand inside the haversack where I kept Misha's knife. I flashed a smile at the soldier and he replied with a faint grimace, I walked in front of him, comforting myself with the thought, 'If he moves or runs after me, I'll stab him in the stomach with my knife.' That *Boche* must have watched me walking away, but I didn't want to look back or start running. If he saw me running like a hunted animal, he would chase me or shoot me in the back. I don't know if that bridge had any strategic importance, probably not, but I was proud of myself for crossing it and for controlling the mind-numbing fear that made my back prickle with every step.

The region I had reached was and still is unfamiliar to me. I crossed it without ever knowing where I was. I walked all day with only my compass to help me find my bearings. I was trying to head west, but insurmountable obstacles prevented me from walking in a straight line. I found myself heading south, then east, and sometimes negotiating steep terrain for ages before I reached flat, open country and houses. Unfortunately, death was still abroad; I could sense it. It was increasingly unusual to see Germans, but there were other, strange black uniforms, emblazoned with crosses. Whenever I came to a village, it would be ruined or abandoned. I wasn't cold any more, but I felt trapped by the mountains I continually had to skirt around. I walked in rivers to soothe my feet. I scaled an enormous rock to find my bearings, then clambered back down, discouraged by the view of the slopes, which dropped away into empty space. I was wearing myself out far more than I had in the forests of Germany or the Ukraine.

The countries I was crossing were at that time called Moldavia and Romania and were still ruled by the pro-Nazi Marshal Antonescu. The mountains that prevented me from heading west were the Carpathians. The valley from which I couldn't escape might have been that of the Siret or Prut rivers — who knows? I tried every direction, day in, day out, but in vain; in the end I was forced to head south.

It felt as if this terrible escape route was never-ending, until finally I reached some flat country which allowed me to walk westwards. For the first time, I'd experienced the fear of being completely lost and that same fear now kept me walking without rest. I began at dawn and collapsed at night. If I was lucky enough to find food, I devoured it on the move. I wanted to escape from there and go home. I had grown up. I was no longer as naïve as I'd been when I left, which is why I was afraid. My nights were filled with nightmares in which I saw only the dead or a breathtakingly deep abyss into which I found myself falling. If I remember less about this period than any other, except for that exhausting walk, it is because I was at a very low ebb. Without putting a name to my condition, I felt as if I were losing heart, both physically and mentally. 'We' are making headway, 'we' will climb . . . my gambit didn't work as well as before. I was crying — I, the little soldier. I didn't even have enough strength to insult my mother's god or beg him for help.

I still spoke to the trees or the birds, whose airborne freedom I envied. Their feet didn't ache. I could have done with a pair of wings to relieve the pain of my wretched feet. I was lucky enough to come across a man with a cart, transporting animal hides; after letting him pass me by, I then followed behind and managed to steal one. Continual drenching in icy water had stiffened my clogs. I made some soles to cushion my feet against the rocky terrain, and when the weather grew milder I walked barefoot.

I came upon a black horse on its own in a pasture, roaming free, without a harness. He was someone to speak to. I murmured to him, telling him he was gentle and beautiful. I couldn't get near enough to stroke him, though, as he kept shying away, so I sat down and waited. This is one of the few clear images I have of this period. The meadow was green, the horse black; it was simply beautiful. Eventually he came over and noisily snuffled at me. I held out a piece of biscuit, which he took. Then I stroked him for a long time, before trying to clamber on to his back. I fell down once, then again and again. He was very big whereas I was small and too exhausted to cling on to his mane. Eventually, though, I managed to hoist myself up flat on my stomach, sliding to one side to reach his neck, which wasn't as broad as his back. I could sit astride there more easily, close to his head. 'Giddy up! Please walk. Carry me.'

I didn't know how to ride a horse or persuade this one to start moving. With my arms around his neck, I spoke softly to him and he eventually began walking — slowly, one step after another, with a regular pace that soothed me — but when he decided to trot, I fell off and had to begin clambering up all over again. I thought I'd be able to sleep on his back while he covered the distance for me. I'd realised that I had to hold on tightly with my legs to avoid slipping off and to pat him on the head to stop him moving too quickly. I slept a little. He walked for a while, then stopped to eat the grass, although I hadn't told him to. As he remained standing and night was falling, I dismounted, leaned against him and dozed standing up myself, before falling fast asleep in the grass. By the time I'd woken up, he had disappeared.

I set off again on my own and eventually came to a railway line, then a small station. I found somewhere to hide so that I could watch the people gathered there. There were still too many soldiers and travellers, both adults and children to risk being seen. The children interested me, since they were as badly dressed as I was and almost as dirty. They would run alongside the carriages, jump on to the step, hold out their hands to the passengers and then bolt, right under the soldiers' noses, like young goats.

After I'd been keeping watch for a long time, a train drew into the station and I saw two kids emerge from beneath a carriage and run away. This was a mode of transport I might be able to use myself — but there were too many soldiers barring my way. I was so exhausted that I was afraid I wouldn't be able to run fast enough to elude capture.

I started walking along the track again to find another station. My only point of reference was the direction taken by the trains: they were coming from the East and were heading west, at last.

The next station, which was quite a distance further on, wasn't as busy. It was small, and there were only a few countrymen there — and no soldiers.

I knew nothing about the design of a train's undercarriage. I thought there'd be a hole or a trapdoor, something that would enable me to hide inside. I ran and hid behind the last carriage of a train that looked suitable, and slipped underneath. All I could see was a long narrow plank suspended under the chassis, just wide enough for me to lie on my stomach on and hold on to the struts of the chassis with both hands. I didn't even have time to consider how dangerous it was, as the train was already pulling out of the station. I quickly tightened my grip — and hell began to flash before my eyes. Stones were thrown up into my face; afraid for my eyes, I made the entire journey with my eyes closed, my body tense, the iron struts cutting into my hands.

The train wasn't fast, like modern trains. The locomotive made a deafening noise and spewed out black smoke. We climbed hills and plunged down the other side, and when I felt the train picking up speed downhill, I'd clench my teeth in terror. I had to hold on tight. If I didn't hold on, I'd had it: I would be crushed by those massive metal wheels. I was so exhausted since leaving the Ukraine that I was having to make a superhuman effort.

I was petrified. Fortunately, I hadn't seen the ground speeding past beneath me, except when the train departed — but I imagined it. Also, I could sense when the train entered a tunnel: the noise became even more deafening and when I risked opening one eye, everything was black.

The train clattered along for a very long time, but doing anything like holding on like that takes so much effort that it might have seemed longer than it actually was. I would guess that my journey took about two hours; we must have covered a fair number of miles. My hands felt as if they were welded to the struts; I had to prise them off to extricate myself when the train stopped — which it did once, enabling me to spit out the dust and rub my nose. My eyes were stinging terribly. I didn't get down, though; I could hear too much noise — including some voices — and I saw boots walking past, so I decided to keep going. I hadn't been crushed to death, the train was doing a lot of mileage on my behalf and, for once, my hands were hurting instead of my feet.

The train set off again and I clenched my

teeth and fists. I don't know how long it was before it finally rumbled to a halt at the next station. By this time I knew I couldn't stand it any longer, and I dropped down between the rails. I was beneath the last carriage, so I was less likely to be seen. Half-blinded, I ran out of the station. I was desperately thirsty; finding myself in a type of marsh, I located a pool of water and plunged my head into it. My hands and face were as black as coal; I used leaves to try to rub them clean.

That mode of transport had been too risky and too exhausting. My hands were shaking and I felt dizzy. Joining the road running alongside another track, I now resigned myself to walking. The next day I was lucky enough to find a locomotive at the head of three or four small carriages stationary in the midst of the countryside. The last carriage was roofless and lined with straw. I decided to make myself comfortable inside and get some sleep. I didn't care where the train was going or when it was due to leave. I was exhausted.

After a moment, I heard voices, but I was well hidden under the straw, so I didn't move. Eventually the small train gently pulled away. I poked my nose out over the straw and saw lush landscapes and fields speeding by. It was very relaxing — I would have enjoyed it if I hadn't been so hungry. The locomotive slowed down as we approached another rural station and I had to hide again.

I could hear some more voices in the distance and the lowing of cattle as they were unloaded. I heard shouts — in a strange language — which sounded nearer, the cattle stamping, and then a whistle blew in the renewed silence and the train pulled out again. I travelled like this for almost a whole day.

I told that train how grateful I was to it for allowing me to rest, for taking pity on my back and feet. If only it could have also provided a little meat! At one point, some more beasts were unloaded, but this time the train didn't set off again; it was the last stop. I waited until the voices had faded, then quickly jumped out before I was caught by anyone coming to unload the straw.

I found something to eat on the trees — a few apples — and even some grapes. Over the days that followed I ventured into villages at nightfall to drink from a fountain, and I'd sleep in a barn or beneath a cart. I was again walking tirelessly, and now I came into more mountain landscapes. My haversack was freshly stocked with meat — an unexpected bonus found hanging in a barn stacked with bottles. I'd assumed it was a leg, because it had a bone through the middle. The flesh was thick and dark but delicious. I'd missed eating meat terribly; now I had a stock that would last for ages. This was a good thing, because that barren, rocky wilderness was enough to drive me to despair. I thought I'd finished with ravines. Bare, treeless rock faces made me scared of falling; I needed at least a bush or two to make me feel safer.

I scaled steep slopes and descended others, I climbed and trudged my way through labyrinths of stone, until my hands and legs were bleeding. I had food, but no water, and it didn't rain often. When it did, I drank any way and as much as I could, with my mouth open, hands outstretched, but on several occasions I had to drink my own urine, squatting down with my hands cupped. I was all alone without any animal company. Animals know how to find water; I didn't.

I hated those mountains. I thought I would die in them. Sometimes I longed to jump into thin air, disappear — no more walking, no more pain, no more dying of thirst. Some of these urges were frighteningly tempting, but the thought of my mother was still there, preventing me from doing anything stupid. I could almost hear her saying, 'I'm waiting for you.'

So I'd back away from the edge. 'No, I can't, I can't; I must go on living.' It all came back to me, that German, all the deaths, the children, and I thought, 'I've survived all that — I must be able to tell my mother, tell her everything I did to find her. We'll have a rest, then we'll keep going.' It was as if I still had a companion, a twin, a wild animal who refused to lie down and die.

The only shelter I found was a sort of cave, reminiscent of the wolves' lair, which I reached with great difficulty. The ravine was sheer and I had to edge along with my back pressed against the rock face. When I finally left the cave, I did so on all fours because my legs were trembling so much. That kind of empty gulf, that feeling of dread, has always been the only thing that really gets to me in the natural world. I've never really managed to overcome that terror. Like my fear of cities and crowds. That cave gave me the chance to rest, eat my fill and sleep. I was craving more and more sleep. I was at the end of my strength. I'd lost count of the number of years I'd been travelling. But my body knew how long it had been, and that last ordeal was almost the end of the road for me. Occasionally I slept in trees, because that hellish land scared me so badly. One morning, I saw a bear. It didn't smell me, the wind can't have carried my scent to him, but what would I have done if he'd attacked? I would probably have used the same method as I had with the wolves, lying motionless on the ground. It would then have been down to how hungry he was. I was later told that he would have sniffed at me and rolled me over with his paws, and if I'd managed to play dead he would have lost interest in me. It's possible. I didn't put the theory to the test.

Countless days and nights passed. Then one day I found myself standing directly above a strange landscape: the sea. Below me was a tiny village. I had managed to come through that hell — and yet the small amount of effort still needed seemed beyond me. I must have been ravenous although I didn't feel hungry; I couldn't see straight and my head felt funny. I was more thirsty than anything else. I drank from a small greenish puddle — I don't know whether it was water. When I found myself further down, a few hundred yards from the village, I felt giddy. I sat down on the ground, unable to move. I had to eat something. I wandered about on the little beach, gathering shells. I chewed their contents after breaking them open with a rock. As I was nearing the village I found better fare: a shed stacked with boxes of larger shellfish. These were harder to open, even with a knife, but they were refreshing and nourishing. After taking a short nap, I sat at the entrance to the village, which was a fishing port clinging to the rocks, with the mountain behind me and the sea stretching out before me.

I was so exhausted — at times virtually unconscious — that I didn't feel like doing anything. I didn't want to hide or to attempt to pilfer anything, even less to ask for help. I think I must have been suffering from malnutrition and dehydration. I could well have been dead in a few days. I also felt disheartened at the sight of all that water. A sea — but which one? On Grandpère's map there had been seas. There had been one in Belgium, but that wasn't the same. I had to do something, but I didn't know what, and I didn't feel capable of doing anything any more. My head was heavy, I felt feverish and my vision was blurred. I could see shadows in the distance on the quay, but I no longer cared.

Gazing out over that infinite expanse of water, I couldn't go any further. That was all I could think: 'I can't go any further.' It was even a relief. It was such an effort to keep my eyes open, and my body felt so odd — I felt numb. I'd been very hungry before — I was capable of going for two or three days without food — but never this hungry. I was skin and bone and my mind had turned to mush.

Through that haze I saw a boat sailing into the dock. I must have been sitting there for a long time, as the light was starting to fade. Then there were people on the quay. A small group — men, women and one or two children. They were talking to a man who had come ashore from the boat. I wasn't very far away, about ten yards, but I couldn't hear very well and the language was completely unfamiliar. It was the sound of a woman's voice that stirred me from my lethargy. It was like music ringing slightly louder than the other voices. It came from a tall, erect figure with blonde hair; she caught my eye because I thought she was beautiful. Several people in the group had glanced at me, without showing any great concern about some girl collapsed on the quay. Few people at that time worried about a dirty, ragged child on her own. But that woman smiled at me. I didn't even have the strength to smile back.

Suddenly she came over and said something to me, but I didn't understand a word. She turned back to the man from the boat, they exchanged several sentences, and she addressed me again. I had a vague feeling she was trying to find a language I would understand. Eventually, her musical, slightly guttural voice said in French, 'What are you doing here? Do you understand French?' She

249

had a heavy accent and spoke quickly, but her French was quite good.

I wasn't even surprised at that. I couldn't have cared less about what was going on around me. They could have captured me and taken me anywhere they wanted; I wouldn't have moved a muscle or opened my mouth. She took my hand a little too vigorously to help me up and I almost fell over. She said kindly, 'It'll be all right. Come on. It'll be all right.'

She made me walk over to the landing stage. I was still in a sort of waking dream. After speaking to the man in the boat, she handed him something sparkling in a handkerchief. I didn't understand what was happening. I found myself on the boat with the others. I remember that we were put in the hold, that someone — probably that woman — gave me something to eat. Then I blacked out as the boat was pulling out of the dock. There was just time to look out of a porthole and get a glimpse of the port, the sea — and then nothing.

When I woke up, it took me a while to work out where I was. There were people sitting on benches and the woman was next to me. I must have slept half lying across her lap. She said, rolling her *rs*, 'You speak Frrrrench! I know you do! You werrrre talking in yourrrr sleep!'

What she was saying seemed strange. I didn't know that you could talk in your sleep. What on earth was she talking about? Was she lying? I was on the defensive again. I kept quiet.

'Do you feel better? Do you want something to eat?'

Still I didn't answer. It was too dangerous; I didn't know where I was. Why had I been brought on to this boat? How long had I been here?

The woman kept talking and gave me something to eat. She didn't seem worried by my silence. The others were also chatting, eating and drinking around us. After giving it some thought, I decided to trust her. I was being fed, I was eating, and that was the main thing. These people had suitcases. They didn't look as though they meant me any harm; they were just passengers.

I couldn't at that time have imagined that I was deep in the hold of an illegal boat with people who were fleeing from Romania, Serbia, Croatia and even Hungary, and had paid a great deal of money to get to Italy. The captain was a smuggler, who must have earned a very good living in those troubled times. That woman's handkerchief had been full of jewellery. People paid with what they

251

had; then they were put ashore somewhere on the coast and it was everyone for themselves.

Why did that woman lumber herself with me? To make herself look as if she were a mother? In the hope of getting preferential treatment? I think I worked out that she'd had a little boy and that she'd been forced to leave him behind. She even wanted me to stay with her.

I refused. The smuggler had put us ashore in an area of marshland, and people were wading about carrying their suitcases. Neither they, nor she, were going my way. I'd heard the magical word '*Italia*' on people's lips: the boot on Grandpère's map and his remark, 'The Italians who run like rabbits.' I've known what he meant by 'run like rabbits' for many years now, but at the time I imagined that the Italians were simply running about all the time — but what were they chasing?

It made no sense to go with that woman. I was now on Grandpère's boot. All I had to do was keep heading north and I would find my mother. The area was muddy, and every step I took sank into the sludge; I ended up walking barefoot until the ground became firmer, then stony.

One day many years later, my husband became fascinated by the idea of retracing my route. I'd left a little port on the Yugoslavian coast, probably near Dubrovnik, and the marshland I'd been wading through was vast enough to be near Comacchio in the province of Ferrara. All the lines drawn by my husband on a map of Europe seemed meaningless, though. A line isn't a bare mountain or a swamp infested with mosquitoes. I wondered then if the harrowing images that haunted my memory might one day take some other form. I still found it terribly hard to talk about them.

9

Another Pack

I'm still guided by smells. I think I've developed a sense that most people barely use. As a child, I simplified the smells of each country I crossed: Germany stank of hatred, Poland of death, and the Ukraine smelled of wolves. All I remember of Yugoslavia was the smell of dry stone. In Italy, there was the continual odour of mud and rain.

After emerging from the marshes, I found myself on one road, then another. Walking was undemanding, almost restful. Food was easy to find compared with my experiences of the past few years. There were German cars on the roads for a time, and some of the villages showed evidence of bombing. I'd never seen so many children, though, and I stopped hiding so frequently because none of those kids seemed afraid of being caught. They were poor, shabbily dressed — like me — and light-fingered; they made me feel less noticeable. I grew bolder with each passing day. I was no longer afraid to soak my feet in a fountain or take food from people's gardens. I merely waited patiently for a woman to hang out her washing, then acquired a pair of trousers or a shirt. I soon looked just like all those kids who were begging audaciously — something I avoided doing for fear of human contact. As soon as anyone came near me, my instinctive reaction was to run away.

I'd regained my strength fairly quickly and my haversack was rarely empty of provisions, mainly fruit and vegetables, as well as some cheese. I was unaccustomed to such abundance. I began to regard Grandpère's Italian boot in a different light. Here, people were poor, but the stables were welcoming, the orchards full of delicious fruit and pilfering easy. So was transport: kids would clamber on to the back of the rickety horse-drawn carts without incurring the owner's wrath. I risked it myself for short distances.

Then, suddenly, in one village, I saw some unfamiliar uniforms, soldiers laughing, chatting to people and handing out sweets. Americans! Children shouted gaily, rushing over to them unabashed to badger them. Was this what an American was, then? Someone who handed out sweets? A friendly soldier?

Grandpère had said that the Americans weren't doing a thing to help us drive out the Germans, but here they were!

The soldiers were standing in a hangar. They gave the women and children packets, cans and cigarettes and, best of all, bars of chocolate. When I saw a child with a chocolate bar, I overcame my wariness and held out my hand as well. That chocolate! I hadn't eaten it very often in Belgium, but there was something wonderful about chocolate. Now, its long-forgotten flavour suddenly flooded my mouth again, leaving me dazed with happiness. I'm still a chocoholic, capable of wolfing down a whole bar of chocolate in a matter of seconds. I involuntarily found myself sitting on a soldier's lap. This tall, beaming fellow opened a tin containing some strange-looking meat and shouted a word out to all and sundry, 'Monkemitte!' — which I memorised phonetically. He wanted me to sample it; he wouldn't take no for an answer. It was soft and didn't taste much like meat, but my stomach welcomed it. Monkey meat! When I was told later that monkey meat was canned beef, a strange feeling came over me. I saw myself sitting on that huge GI's lap, indiscriminately devouring chocolate, meat, sweets and biscuits like the other kids, and that man roaring with laughter as he fed us.

He seemed genuinely happy.

The Germans had gone. I could walk fearlessly across a country that had in places been decimated, but was now free. Freedom from the Germans still tastes like chocolate and Monkemitte to me. Obviously the rest of my route through Italy wasn't strewn with chocolate. I resumed my pilfering, now from markets where provisions were scarce, then resigned myself to begging like the other children. At first, I'd thought that there was plenty of food, but the further north I travelled the hungrier people seemed to be, and the more sparsely stocked the stalls. The stallholders didn't trust kids. I longed for some bread, but there was none to be had anywhere. I didn't see any meat at all.

On one occasion, I managed to pick up some sandals; they were my size, but they didn't fit my feet well enough for me to run — and I had to be able to run after each attempted theft, whether I'd succeeded or not.

Whenever I heard French spoken, I acted the idiot. One day, as a farmer and his rickety cart were overtaking me along a narrow mountain track, he suddenly asked, 'Where are you off to, *petite?*'

I hadn't spoken for years, except to myself, the animals and trees, and sometimes to the sky or Death. I had been more or less struck dumb. In order to reply to the farmer, I had first to string the words together in my head. He must have thought I had a stutter, or that he was talking to a simpleton. 'I'm — I'm going . . . to see my parents.'

'And where are your parents?'

'In the north.'

'Climb up then!'

Strangely enough, I could understand him perfectly. It was just that when I replied the words got stuck. I needed time to formulate each reply, and producing long sentences was out of the question. It didn't really bother me, though, as speaking was no longer my forte. It didn't prevent me from thinking or calculating my chances of going faster. I didn't realise what I'd become in almost four years of wandering: a scrawny, feral child with a scarred face and body. It didn't occur to me that I might scare people. I felt as if I'd grown up.

My hair, which I'd trimmed with a knife, was tucked under my hat. The last jacket I'd stolen was too long and my frayed boy's trousers were dirty, but the kids I'd seen in Italy had been far more tattered. That kind man took me some distance in his cart. There were many farms and fields and I had a good view from that dirt track of little valleys and copses of trees. I also travelled by cart one other time and was given a crust of bread when we came to a farm.

My vocabulary was too limited, though. When people asked me where I was going or why I was out walking so late, I found it hard to reply and anyway was afraid to explain. I withdrew into my shell. I waved goodbye and that was all. I didn't even ask where I was; I'd got out of the habit. I just kept walking. I kept thinking about my mother and was anxious to be back on familiar ground so that I could look for her there, in Belgium. As far as I was concerned, it was all very simple: Papa and Maman were bound to be on their way back from the East, like me. I'd seen the Americans and I thought the war was over. That wasn't yet the case.

I remember one road in particular where I took a wrong turn: at a crossroads I mistakenly turned right instead of left. This brought me to a large gate, which I initially thought was the entrance to a château. It was actually a convent, and the road stopped there.

It was foggy, I'd been walking for a very long time and I didn't want to retrace my steps. I was furious at the idea of wasting my time. I'd wanted to forge ahead quickly and instead I'd come to a deadend. I decided to knock on the door.

It was opened by a nun.

'I'm hungry.'

'Come in.'

I walked through large rooms with high ceilings and archways in the walls. There was a refectory at the end of a long corridor.

'What are you doing out on the road so late?'

'I'm going to see my parents. I lost my way, so I'm hungry.'

'Sit down over there. I'll bring you something to eat.'

She came back with a bowl of warm milk, a slice of bread and a few vegetables. I wasn't the only person staying there. A group of young men were also eating and there were mattresses on the floor. The place must have been used by travellers as a stopover. It was by listening to the young men's conversation that I learned the war wasn't yet over in the north, although they sounded full of hope. The next day, after a good night's sleep, I followed the sisters around for a while until they fed me again. The war wasn't over, so I had to stock up on food.

Later on, when I had the chance to return to France as an adult, I thought that the countryside around Grenoble resembled what I recalled of that convent's surroundings. The roads looked familiar. I had a feeling of déjà vu; I'd seen that scenery before. I never did find it, though: the convent at the end of a mountain road where they'd been so kind to me.

Knowing that the *Boches* were still in the area with their rifles, boots and *vert-de-gris* uniforms, I should have turned round. The Americans hadn't driven all of them out. What else could I do, though, except keep heading for Belgium and then find Grandpère? He would know where my mother was. He was bound to have some news.

I'd certainly grown bigger, but my frame of mind hadn't altered much since I'd first left. I was just as stubborn when it came to my obsession: Maman. I still had a mental age of seven and was just as afraid of being caught by the Virago. I never ever wanted to see that woman again. I thought about her as I made my way through the forest which was leading me back to Grandpère. I talked to her: 'Look what this Boeotian managed to do. You'd never have managed it! But I did. I left and now I've come back — but not to you.'

Some of the old feelings of resentment resurfaced: the day she'd had her husband's old cat put down. It was a sick, mangy old cat, who just wanted to end his days curled up in an armchair. Then there were her remarks: 'Your mother? Where's your mother now?' 'If the Germans win, we'll hand her over to them.' I hadn't been able to forgive or forget.

What I remember about that journey through France was a feeling of relief. Hearing my native language again, seeing those familiar landscapes. I could breathe again. I felt as if I were coming home.

Finally, one day, I found myself walking along a road in Belgium when I heard someone shouting, 'Hey, is that you?' and someone else replying, 'Yeah.' That 'Yeah' was said with a Belgian accent. I was home.

When I saw the signpost on the road to Brussels, I quickened my pace. I felt proud, and couldn't wait to rush into Marthe's and Grandpère's arms. I turned my back on the church near the Virago's house and dashed along the path to the farm — then stopped, disorientated. I looked for the fence and the sheep, but all I could see was the fence. I should have been able to see the trees, the roof of the farm, but there was nothing. I retraced my steps, searching my childhood memories, but they stopped at that fence. I walked round and round, but the farm was gone. I couldn't have made a mistake. I knew that road by heart.

I wept in despair. What should I do now?

Where should I go? The Virago might know where Grandpère was, but I wasn't going to risk my neck at her house. She might lock me up. Grandpère had disappeared — perhaps he was dead. Had the farm been bombed by those wretched planes? I couldn't see any ruins. There was nothing but emptiness, a wasteland, no sign of the chickens, sheep and dogs, or the swing.

I started walking along the canal in the opposite direction to put as much distance as possible between me and that neighbour-hood. I dawdled about in a square looking for something to eat, then started to search for somewhere to spend the night. Coming to a vast hilly, wooded area with a lake, I climbed some small wooden steps to another path, which gave me a perfect view of the neighbourhood from its highest point. I had shelter and I could hide in the trees, and so, sadly, I went about the business of restructur-ing my life. I found out when the market was held and swiped what I needed — potatoes, a blanket. I was lonely and miserable.

'Hey, what did you just nick? I saw you!'

'Go away!'

'It's not terribly clever to do it all on your own. We have a house and we share.' The boy was plump, curly-haired, fair and not as ragged as I was. He'd pronounced the word 'house' with an air of importance. I must have looked enviously at him, because he added, 'I'm Sigui! Do you want to see our house?'

I wasn't afraid to follow him. My hand was still in my haversack, clutching the knife I'd found in the woods before reaching Brussels. I was very fond of its carved wooden handle. I also had the blade of a Russian bayonet, so I felt well armed.

Anyway, I was leading a miserable existence and had been on my own for weeks or months. I'd watch people going home, children with parents. Sometimes I'd stand outside a front door for ages. I'd tried to remember the address of the house where my parents' apartment had been. On one occasion, I almost circled Brussels entirely to find that tramway, but the line was long and my compass useless in city streets. I'd never been told whether I lived in the north or the south. All I knew was the outskirts of the city, near the ruined bridge and Grandpère's farm. I had put enough distance between me and that area to feel confident I could avoid meeting the Virago, and I stayed there because I knew various landmarks, like the church, the market square and the canal. I was on the move virtually all day long keeping body and soul together, and at night I lay low in the park.

The house commandeered by Sigui and his gang stood further away on what was at that time called the 'plateau', overlooking the park. On the way there, he told me he was part of a gang and that they managed very well together, stealing from market stalls and shop displays. They then shared the loot. In his opinion, it was smarter and more efficient: 'We've got everything we need. We're warm and comfortable. You don't have to worry. The more of us there are, the better we'll get by.'

I didn't say a word. I was feeling intimidated by this unexpected contact with a teenager older than me. He was offhand, very much at ease, streetwise. He couldn't have known that I'd barely emerged from my chaotic childhood. He'd spotted me easily and had taken me for an inexperienced runaway when he saw me nicking a measly spud from a stand.

The house had been deserted for a long time. They called it 'the house of spiders'. From the outside, it was white and square, and there was a terrace where they sunbathed. Entrance was through a window, and inside it was completely empty. They had spread blankets on the floor in a spacious ground-floor room, the shutters were closed and there were spiders everywhere, hanging from the windows, the corners of doors, the ceiling.

He showed me the things they'd pilfered: bottles of water, glass bottles of milk and all kinds of provisions. They put candles in the empty hearths to light the rooms. If they wanted to wash, they had to go to the lake in the park or to a neighbouring farmer, who had a pump. 'The girls go over to that bloke's house, but you can do what you want.'

I didn't see 'the girls' on that first day, but he introduced me to the others. There was 'the Canadian', 'Mouton' and 'the Gorille'. The Canadian, the eldest, was a young gangster in a jacket, who looked afraid of nothing. Mouton had a sad, pale, thin face, curly black hair which was much too long and sweeping eyelashes. The Gorille was small, stocky and must have been at least eighteen. I was awed by the older boys, but I felt more drawn to Mouton. Particularly when the Canadian said, 'He's a bit strange, you know, but don't take any notice. His parents were killed right in front of him.' Mouton didn't go hunting outside, because the Canadian, who had been born not in Canada but in Belgium, was very protective. Sigui was by far the most cunning. With his bright eyes and wide, slightly mocking grin, he organised the looting raids to supply what the gang needed.

There were two girls, who arrived a little later. The first was Margot, a beautiful brunette with an impressive chest and a shrill voice, who 'got by' in her own way, according to Sigui: 'She helps herself at the local farmer's house. She has some very convincing arguments up her sleeve!' She was seventeen or eighteen, and didn't like the boys teasing her, which they often did, about her 'pillows'. The Gorille would say, 'Any chance of sleeping on your pillows?' The other girl, Denise, was a thin brunette with short hair, a comical little face and buck teeth. She was never at a loss for words and the boys didn't pester her.

I wonder what I looked like in the midst of that small gang of crooks, skilled at shoplifting and survival. I wasn't like them. But I did begin to talk a little about myself. I began by telling them my name, Mishke. They didn't ask any questions and nor did I. Apart from Mouton's tragedy, I never knew anything about any of them — where they had come from or if they had family anywhere. We talked about food, clothing and the basics we needed to survive.

As I was the youngest, I was never given any specific jobs. The Canadian, Sigui and the Gorille would go out 'hunting', but before they left they'd always come to an agreement.

'I've seen some jackets and hats.'

'I've seen a stall with some cheese.'

First they pinpointed anything easy to take, then they worked out what we needed. They had a tried and tested technique. One of them went over to ask something and while the shopkeeper was busy explaining, the other would steal. Two or three of them would go if the job was difficult — if a street was too wide or not crowded enough for them to make their getaway without being seen. Everyone had their part to play; then we'd bring back what we'd acquired and share it out. I was given cheese, apples, bread, sometimes margarine, pig fat, which I loved, and bacon. On a few occasions, they brought me back some little jackets, which were often too short or too long. We all needed jackets and blankets, which weren't easy to pinch. I was also given a shawl. Shoes were trickier. I held on to some clogs made from a rubbery material for ages. They were practically my size and came up above the ankle. That winter, as I recall, I wore my first pair of socks in years. I didn't like socks, but the clogs weren't very warm and socks were very easy to pilfer. Everyone had some. I often slept while they were off stealing. I was more than happy not to be roaming the streets any more. All that mattered was being able to eat my fill. I was always hungry. I've spent my whole life feeling hungry.

My closest relationship was with Mouton. We'd hold hands. He rarely spoke. My vocabulary was very limited anyway. I didn't express myself well and used phrases a little girl might use. I couldn't remember many words and I didn't know the correct meaning of some of them. I hadn't developed. I felt as if I knew how to talk but that someone had put a lid on that knowledge and nothing would come out. I knew what I wanted to say but I didn't know how to say it. The words just wouldn't come. Mouton's silences were a great comfort to me, because with him I could at least make the attempt without anyone poking fun at me.

I experienced terrible difficulties when I was made to go to college later on. I'd lost contact completely with society and its language, as well as with what passed for 'normal' behaviour. There were so many things I could have and would have said, but I didn't know how. What I wanted to say to Mouton was, 'I've suffered too, you know. I wandered all over the world and still didn't manage to find my parents. We have to go on living. We'll help each other. We're in this together. You mustn't lose heart, we have to keep going.' I would have liked at least to describe a few childhood memories which might have comforted us both.

I didn't know who in the gang was Jewish and who wasn't. It wasn't a problem for us. We lived at one remove from society, on the fringes, just as I'd lived on the outskirts of the forests with my wolves. Some of us went hunting and everyone benefited and that was a good thing. I didn't question Mouton; he looked too ill. He would cough loudly, but we didn't have anything to make him feel better. He often had a temperature and the Canadian would wrap him in a blanket. Margot went to the farm and asked her farmer for a cup of milk with some honey to give him some relief, but that meagre remedy didn't do much to help. I think he must have been suffering from tuberculosis.

The Canadian didn't want Mouton to go hunting outside so he was excluded from their plans of attack, as were the girls. Sometimes I thought being left out was an easy option, but at other times it irritated me. I knew I was physically capable of pulling off my own raids, but I wasn't the one who devised the plans for finding the targets — although I could have put my observation skills and keen grasp of strategy to good use. My job was petty theft, because I was small. I fumed in silence: I would have liked to tell them how to do it, but I didn't have the right words. I always stole the same thing: food, like a box of pig fat. I didn't even know what I was taking sometimes; I just brought back anything — someone was bound to enjoy it. The first time, I dipped my fingers into the box of pig fat for a taste, I was so used to eating alone. The others taught me the laws of communal living: anything brought back was shared.

Sigui was the most handsome boy in the gang. He used to flirt with Denise. They'd dance to the scratchy music of an old wind-up gramophone. I watched them kissing and thought it was odd. I hadn't yet become a woman; that didn't happen until much later. My body had adapted to my living conditions — it was tough, battered and boyish. I knew I wasn't pretty. It was easy to compare myself with the others. My bust was virtually non-existent, I was thin and I didn't yet understand that sort of relationship between a girl and a boy. As a result, it was strange watching the others kissing. It was like an unfamiliar game.

I felt at ease with the others, but they were humans and I was still on my guard. My animal survival instinct, which had stood me in good stead during my years of wandering, continued to protect me. I enjoyed comparing

271

knives; I was pleased every time I managed to steal one from somewhere. I didn't know how to survive without a knife, without biting and without scraping away at my skin like a troublesome shell.

One day, Félix, the Gorille, tried to grab me. I had a pretty good idea why, but he soon realised it wasn't a good idea to cross swords with me. All he got for his trouble were some hefty blows. He flung me to the ground to have his way, pulling at my trousers. He was very strong, but so was I. If I hadn't fought back, I think he would have raped me. I bit, scratched and pummelled him until his nose was bleeding. He can't have expected a scrawny kid like me to put up so much resistance.

I was shaking all over after that. I don't know whether it was fear, the memory of something else or the excitement of the scuffle, but I took myself off to a corner to recover. As soon as he came within a few feet of me, I stiffened, backing away instinctively. Sigui noticed, understood and solved the problem diplomatically: 'Leave the girl alone. Look elsewhere. We're a gang. I don't want any problems with her.'

Margot wanted to fix the place up a little and make it more attractive. She'd brought back a very tall plant with a few leaves right at the top, which Denise made fun of, saying she thought it was pathetic. She also made fun of Margot's plans to move into the farmer's house. Every time she saw her slipping off to visit him, her bust swaying back and forward under her blouse, Denise sniggered with the others, 'So when's the wedding?'

'You can laugh, but you don't refuse his grub!' retorted Margot. Everyone knew she was right. The farmer made our meals at 'the house of spiders' a little more interesting.

All in all it was a good life. Sometimes we sunbathed on the terrace with its wonderful view over the park, like little bourgeois billionaires! I preferred throwing knives on the plateau with the boys, though. We'd aim at trees, and I was very good. One day I was stupid enough to show them my bayonet blade with its characteristic triangular point, designed to cause wounds that wouldn't heal. It was much harder to throw. We were so engrossed in our game that no one noticed the copper. The police didn't usually say anything to us as we were only playing there, but it was another matter when he saw the Russian bayonet. I didn't want to tell him it was mine; I was too frightened of being dragged off to prison. The Canadian, who was the eldest, immediately said, 'It's mine,' whereupon the copper took him and the Russian bayonet off to the police station.

The Canadian came back without the bayonet. He'd been forced to tell some story about finding it — but I'd just lost something very precious to me. That bayonet had come from so far away, from that field of dead soldiers in the Ukraine where I'd gathered my stars. All I had left in my haversack was my compass, which I didn't show them, my stars and my knife from the Ardennes.

We often organised little parties, when the Gorille had gone gallivanting about, looking for girls. Margot and Denise would light candles and we'd spread a sheet on the floor, laid with some pilfered treats — a few biscuits, a bottle of beer or wine, anything we had that was special. If we couldn't share the last delicacy, we gambled for it. If all we had left was a bottle of beer, for example, then we needed two winners. Everyone would put one hand behind their back, choose a number between one and five with their fingers, then show it to the others. I don't remember what the winning order was, but I drank the beer once and didn't like it — it was too bitter. I'm very fond of it now, though; it's the taste of Belgium. I preferred to play for biscuits, pig fat or roast chestnuts. Anything sweet.

These parties were much like a family

get-together really. The Gorille was the only one of us who'd risk going out at night. The others didn't want to be seen. We all had our reasons, but deep down we felt the same: we didn't get on with people. They went about their business, their work, they went to school, they were the 'bourgeoisie' or the 'bigots'. Their children were nothing like us, and we cherished that difference. It meant freedom. We knew nothing, or at least I didn't, about how the war was progressing. The Canadian might have done; he was more mature — and his pilot's jacket must have come from somewhere. He knew what had happened to Mouton's parents, but didn't talk about it. He wasn't afraid of the coppers either. We were. If we decided to go walking in the countryside when it was hot, we took great pains not to draw attention to ourselves. We were abandoned kids, with no family, and none of us wanted to wind up at the police station. Only the Canadian didn't seem to be frightened of anything.

The boys brought us news of the outside world, but they talked mainly about markets, livestock shows or clothing stalls. One day, though, Sigui came back saying that we had to go and look, as something was going on in the town. People were celebrating in the streets. As we drew nearer to the village centre, more and more flags were appearing at the windows. We followed a crowd who seemed to be making for the same place, the chaussée de Mons, where I watched the arrival of my first liberating tank. The English.

Sigui lifted me up to sit on a windowsill. I was above the crowd and I began to cry. Everyone was happy. People were shouting, jumping for joy, and I felt abandoned. Deeply sad. Where were my parents? During all that time I had been hoping to see them. They had been alive in a bubble in a corner of my mind and I realised, on that Armistice Day, as the bells pealed and everyone in Belgium celebrated, that there was no happiness in store for me. I had lost them. If they had come looking for me, they would only have gone to the farm. I didn't think my parents would have turned up at the Virago's house. Only Grandpère knew my mother. He'd talked to me about her. I had 'pretty ears, just like her'. I was convinced that Grandpère held the key to everything, but the farm was gone. Armistice was one more disappointment.

Mouton wasn't with us. He must have felt sad too. Much later that year, we heard rumours and the Canadian said, 'People are coming back from the East. They're very thin.

It's not a pretty sight.' So I started roaming the streets, looking at passers-by, but the way they regarded us street urchins had begun to change. They called us 'vermin': 'Get the hell out of here, vermin!' Once, I thought I saw my father. An emaciated face, blond hair. That man looked so thin and so sad. I studied his face and he didn't even notice me. Before Armistice Day, I hadn't looked at people; they had nothing to do with me. After that day, though, I couldn't stop looking at them. I still lived in hope and although my legs had stopped roaming the earth to find my parents, my eyes still sought them in every face.

Mouton was in low spirits, but no one realised how depressed he was, because he was always sad and ill. I was very fond of him. One day, we were sitting on the floor in the large room with its spiders, holding hands. It was a beautiful day outside.

'Wouldn't you like to go up on the roof?'

'No, I'd prefer to stay here.'

'OK, we'll stay here, then.'

'You don't wear a chain around your neck, do you?' (Margot had a pretty chain that the farmer had given her.)

'No, I haven't got one.'

Mouton rummaged around in his pocket. 'Would you like this?'

'Oh! That's pretty!' It was a little green Buddha hanging from a metal chain. It was completely worthless, but it was green and I loved green. I put it on immediately and kissed Mouton. To my eyes, that cheap piece of jewellery, probably stolen from a market, was much prettier than Margot's chain.

Mouton had given me his last gift. One dreadful afternoon, as I was coming back from the village, I saw Sigui running out of the house. 'Wait!' he commanded. 'Wait. Don't go in! Something's happened!'

'What's wrong?'

'Wait, I said!' He looked really upset.

The Canadian was behind me. Sigui took him to one side to speak to him and he immediately rushed into the house. I ran in behind him and Sigui couldn't stop me.

Mouton had hanged himself from a beam. The Canadian was sobbing loudly as he took him down. I fell to my knees beside them and we all cried with incomprehension and rage. He'd been left on his own, which was unusual, and he'd made the most of the opportunity to leave us behind, to be united with death. It seemed so unfair. Everyone felt to blame, particularly the Canadian, who had loved him like a kid brother and had been so protective of him. I understood then why he'd kept such a close watch on him.

I don't know who decided to inform the police. Margot, probably. It must have been her because she ran off to the farmer's house and the coppers arrived soon after. Mouton's death meant the end for us. By leaving the gang, he destroyed it. The Canadian was devastated. It was awful to see a boy so tough and so full of himself crying with such wracking sobs. I was shaking all over; the yawning emptiness was waiting to swallow me. The protection I'd enjoyed from the gang for almost a year had suddenly vanished, as if the house had gone up in smoke. Everything had been so warm before, so affectionate, and now it was over. I felt cold to the core.

Two police cars took us to the police station. The Canadian didn't want to leave Mouton. He refused to go and fought with the policemen.

'Don't worry, son, we'll take care of him. Come on, lad.' They were kind men. They were just trying to understand what had happened and they didn't mean us any harm.

The Canadian managed to clamber into the car, holding Mouton wrapped in a sheet. I never saw him again.

Once we arrived at the police station, we were separated. I found myself standing before a kindly superintendent, who wanted to know my name and what I was doing in that squat. 'Mishke? What does Mishke mean? Don't you know your parents' surname?'

'No.'

'Where do you come from, dressed like that?'

'Er, from the war.'

'OK. Listen. We'll pop over to the Town Hall and see if there's any trace of you, but if you don't have any relatives, we'll have to sort this out. You must go to school and have someone to take care of you! Don't you know anyone?'

'No.'

So he said, 'Wait here. I'll bring you something.'

He was a good man. He came back with a cup of hot chocolate and some bread and butter.

'Eat this. Take your time. I'll be back.'

When he came back, he told me that there was a lady who was keen to take care of me, that this would make everyone happy, that I would have a family and that I shouldn't worry.

'All right, but can I see the others?'

'Not right now. Later. You'll see each other again, but not now. For now, we'll go over to see that lady. OK?'

He drove me to the lady's house. She was a

smartly dressed middle-class woman in high heels. 'You realise,' she said to him, 'that this is moving a little fast. I've been making arrangements as quickly as I can . . . but she can sleep on the sofa and then we'll see.'

On the sofa . . . again! I was going to end up on the sidelines as I had been at the Virago's house.

The kindly superintendent must have seen my expression, but I don't think he changed his mind as quickly as he did just because of that. He must've taken a dislike to the lady. 'Listen, Madame, if you don't have a bed yet, I have two other people who'd be glad to have her. A couple of schoolteachers, so they can take care of her education at the same time as giving her board and lodging.'

'Fine. If that would be better, all well and good. You're bound to have another child to place.'

We went back to the police station. That nice man explained that I'd be living with 'two good ladies, devout Catholics, who will take care of your upbringing'. He said he was going to inform them immediately, and that I'd be sleeping in a bed that night.

I waited in his office, with my haversack which I hadn't wanted to put down. I still had my knife, my compass and my stars, and my little green Buddha around my neck. My only possessions. Then Grandpère walked in.

I threw myself at him. This was the most wonderful present in the world. He was here. He would take me with him and tell me where my parents were. I didn't ever want to let him go.

Grandpère had been told I was there by staff at the Town Hall, former colleagues. He'd been trying to find me for ages and when he'd been told that the police had rounded up a gang with a little blonde girl, he'd come to take a look. This wasn't the first time he'd come here to inspect the kids who'd been picked up in the streets. There were more than you might have imagined after the war. He'd been disappointed on many occasions, but this time he'd found me. He had given my name, the one I hated: Monique Valle. I had been identified. They had found evidence of my fake birthday of 12 May 1937 in Brussels. Grandpère didn't say anything more to the superintendent, though, whom he appeared to know, except that I didn't have any parents.

'Where are Papa and Maman?'

'You have to get used to the idea, *mon coco* . . . No one knows.'

'Am I staying with you, then? Can we go now?'

'I would've liked that, *mon coco*, but the

superintendent says I'm too old and that he's found some kind ladies who'll take care of you and teach you so that you can go to college.'

'Will you come and see me?'

'If I'm allowed to, I will.'

'What about Marthe?'

'She's gone, *mon petit coco*. She was very ill and she died.'

I had been hoping that Marthe would plait my hair, make a fuss of me, wash me in the basin and make me some nice new clothes. I was more disappointed than genuinely upset; I'd seen so many dead people. I didn't know what to say. It was hard to imagine Grandpère without Marthe — and I didn't understand why I couldn't live with him. He'd aged, he looked tired, but he was still the Grandpère I'd known, albeit without his familiar strength and cheerfulness.

'So, where did you run off to like that? You seem to have got yourself into a nice mess.'

'I must tell you all about it, Grandpère! I walked a very long way, miles and miles. I was in the East.'

'Later. Tell me all about it later. You are a funny little thing!'

Later! It was always too late for me. I hated those 'later's. I still had my compass. I wanted to tell him everything I'd done with it. But

Grandpère didn't like displays of emotion; a few years later, I realised that this was just his nature.

He spoke very little about Marthe. When I asked him how she'd died, he replied, 'She had to go into the hospital. She was spitting blood.' No details. He refused to feel sorry for anyone, even himself. He didn't want to stir up old memories.

Many years later, when we were finally able to live together, he'd spend his days in an armchair by the window, gazing into space and smoking his pipe. When our meal was ready, he would eat in silence. When I wanted to talk, he'd say, 'At home, when I was living with my parents, my father had a cap and if anyone tried to talk at the table he'd pick up that cap and bang it on the table; we had to eat in silence.' So he ate in silence, but the great silence of old age was new to me.

I never heard him talk about his son. He'd always respected Marthe's grief, but he'd wanted her to forget. Just as I should forget: 'Take it easy, *mon coco*. Move on and don't look back. Everything will be OK, you'll go to school. The past is dead and buried.'

'Hey, Grandpère, wait! Look! I kept it! I still have the compass!'

'So you still have that little thing, do you?' As if it wasn't at all important, that shiny little object which I'd carried in my mouth for years across thousands of miles.

'You will come and see me, won't you?'

'Of course. Of course.'

He wasn't able to for many years, though. The two women who were to put me up didn't want anything to do with him and his 'bad influence'. Grandpère was a kind of anarchist who didn't have any truck with priests or the Church. He had no place in the new upbringing that was in store for me, a feral child who had to be tamed and brought back into the social fold.

10

A Pet Rat for Company

Léontine and Sybil welcomed me into their neat, impeccably polished house willingly, if a little cautiously. With one eye on my haversack and the other on my neck. 'What have you got in there?'

'Some biscuits.'

'And that?'

'That's my little god.'

'Oh, no! We can't have that!'

They took my green Buddha away from me. I was allowed only one god and that was theirs. I hung on to my haversack, though, determined they wouldn't take that from me.

'It's disgusting. Look how dirty it is. We'll wash it for you.'

'All right — but not today!'

'Very well! We'll wash it later, then.'

They seemed to think that a filthy haversack was not as serious as my little Buddha, so I had time to hide my knives, compass and stars. The next day my haversack was washed and stripped of its significance. It hung over my chair, no longer a symbol of my adventures, remaining empty until I used it to carry my schoolbooks.

I changed the hiding place for my treasures every day. The high bed had two mattresses laid one on top of the other, which allowed me to hide my knives in the gap between them. My first-floor room had a small washbasin, a window overlooking a tiny garden and a tall cupboard, the bottom drawer of which was for my things. They gave me some little blouses, a skirt, a sweater, some panties and a long-sleeved floral-patterned nightdress with a ridiculous collar.

I was a real problem for those ladies, though, when it came to shoes. They'd examined my feet with interest, unable to come up with an explanation for their morphology. 'My goodness! What on earth is this? Are you ill? She must have some disease. What caused this?'

'I've been walking for a very long time.'

'No, that can't be it. This is a disease!'

I think they mentioned poliomyelitis, but I'm not sure whether I'm remembering such a complicated word correctly; in their eyes, I was deformed as a result of some disease. As I was in pain all the time, I inherited a pair of hand-me-down sandals which, despite being my size, were too narrow to accommodate my toes. I had developed the habit of clenching my toes to protect myself and over time they had become deformed. Although I sometimes managed to stretch them straight, as soon as I took my shoes off they resumed their former bent position. In addition to that, the callused skin on my soles was as hard as leather. These orphan-girl feet completely flummoxed the two spinsters, who had no choice but to have shoes made to measure for me.

Years later I was given an operation. Among the other torments inflicted, I had to have an iron rod inserted in my big toe because it was so far away from the others. It was as if I had a sixth finger; it was practical for climbing and gripping, but not for everyday life. In the meantime, as soon as I came of age, I began wearing very high heels that forced my toes flat, although I had to put up with agonising pain when I took off my shoes and my stretched tendons snapped back into position. When I was living with Léontine and Sybil, though, wearing high heels was out of the question. I had flat sandals and I tended to walk rather heavily, like an automaton.

The first evening, when they sent me to bed, I was overcome by a fit of blind terror, which they thought had come out of the blue. They had just covered me with a blanket. 'Take it off! I don't want it! It stinks of death.' Huddled against the bedhead, I put all my strength into pushing away that threadbare, colourless thing which really did smell of death. I'd recognise that stench anywhere. The blanket had been wrapped around a corpse. 'It stinks of death!'

'No, it doesn't! Léontine, where did we get that blanket?'

'From the old people's home — but it's been washed.'

Washed or not, it stank of death, and they had to give me a blanket from their own cupboard. They explained about brushing my teeth with white powder and showed me the toilet on the ground floor — which didn't stop me from climbing out of the window and jumping into the garden to answer the call of nature.

In any case, I was upset with them for taking Mouton's little Buddha away from me. That had suited me fine as a god. But it was only when they forced me to pray and to go to church that I spoke to them about my genuine difference from them. 'But I'm Jewish!'

'No, you're not. Your name is Monique.'

'Mishke! My name's Mishke!'

There was nothing to be done. The Town Hall had provided information about the orphan I was and, to top it all, I was blonde. As far as they were concerned, I could only be Belgian and Catholic.

I cried a great deal for my mother during that period of apprenticeship. The little Buddha was dead and gone. Those two women wanted to wash me, teach me, discipline me, peel off my wolf skin. Their world was narrow and incomprehensible and I missed my parents badly. I had no time for that tiny garden with its two solemn apple trees standing in the midst of a patch of grass. I felt choked by the thought of the freedom that had been stolen from me. They locked me in my room at night to prevent me from stealing jam from the kitchen cupboard or peeing in the garden. I was well fed, with good bread, warm milk and meat, so why should I steal jam? I had to learn everything. Those elderly spinsters just wanted to help me, but we were worlds apart.

Although officially ten, I was actually three years older, but my academic standard was that of an eight-year-old. I read falteringly, letter by letter, I could barely write, I counted on my fingers and, apart from certain notions about geography which we didn't learn in class, I was completely ignorant. But that void was soon filled. They made me work every day on a massive table in a room next to my bedroom. I've never seen a table as big as that one since. Léontine worked, Sybil worked and I worked. They marked their pupils' homework, while I endeavoured to learn how to write letters, then words, properly. They skipped very quickly from one subject to another. Reading, writing, counting and reciting fables by heart. Their technique was to read stories to me, then make me read them myself and finally copy them out word for word.

I was an unusually fast learner. I had an excellent memory and made rapid scholastic progress. Only social adaptation remained impossible. I was rough, impulsive and occasionally violent and I continually rebelled. When I came across *Little Red Riding Hood*, I flew into a memorable rage and flung the book across the room, calling them lunatics!

'Why did you do that?'

'This is rubbish. It makes no sense at all!'

'What do you mean?'

'There's no such thing as a wolf who eats children! It's not true!'

'It's just a story!'

'I don't care. I don't want it. It's not true!'

'Very well. Calm down. We'll look at

291

something else.' I was given *Tom Thumb, The Bluebird*, which I loved, and *Sleeping Beauty*. Soon I knew them all by heart. Then I was given a little dictionary: 'When you've learned everything in there, you'll be very clever indeed.'

I loved that. I passed from one word to another, thought about the meanings and asked hundreds of questions. I still found it very hard to string sentences together; I'd used spoken language with a limited vocabulary for too long. But because they had promised that if I made up for lost time I'd be able to go to college — outside — I made very fast progress. I was in a rush to write. I thought that if I didn't write things down, I'd forget — and I didn't want to forget. That poor dying man had said, 'Don't forget.'

The spinsters didn't ask any questions about my past. I couldn't be Jewish, and my parents were dead, but no one wanted to know how. Léontine and Sybil were 'brides of God' — that was how they'd explained their spinsterhood to me. God came up continually, at lunch, tea and dinner; I thought their husband terribly intrusive. 'But I'm Jewish! My mother was Jewish.'

'No, you're not.' They had a brother who was a priest, and their conversation was firmly focused on my future. 'You'll go to

292

college, you'll become a teacher and you'll earn your living.' I suppose they'd also thought I might enter the convent, but they must have given up that idea soon enough.

I began at teaching college when I was about sixteen, wearing knee-length cotton panties, a woollen skirt, a blouse buttoned up to the neck and flat sandals. I looked hideous and I knew it. I'd talk to myself in the evening in my room, because I hadn't yet gained the skill to write as fast as I spoke. Those old-fashioned panties drove me wild. I took them off in front of all the other girls and threw them into the stairwell at the college. You rebel any way you can. Unfortunately, they bought me some more and I came in for their frequently repeated lecture castigating loose women! I also mentioned lipstick, which the others wore and I thought looked pretty.

'Girls wearing lipstick? That's disgusting!'

'Do you want to know what's really disgusting? Shall I tell you what I saw?'

'No! The things you talk about are terrible!'

The two spinsters were there just to lecture me, educate me, turn me into a good person. It made me think, 'Aren't I a good person, then? Why doesn't anyone care about the pain I went through? Why am I forced to look ugly when the other girls wear pretty clothes?'

Some of them wore make-up but I, with my scarred face, wasn't allowed. My hideous feet, my sturdy legs, covered with scars, and my hair! I'd forgotten my hair. I had fine, thin, flyaway hair which was so unruly that I never managed to smooth it down, even when I dampened it.

I looked a fright — and they, instead of trying to tidy me up, made me look ridiculous. One day, they presented me with a hat. I tried refusing to wear it, but there was nothing to be done: they thrust it on to my head. None of the other students had a hat, so I announced that if the wind blew it off, I wouldn't run after it. I stood up straight, I turned the corner of the street and the wind caught the rim of the hat and carried it away. Sybil ran after it, but I had won: after that I had to wear it only to church.

Church was another mystery. The house of God, who was there only in spirit. I didn't want any holy water either — I was Jewish! It didn't matter; they dipped my hand in it anyway. I had to learn the prayers by heart, reciting texts I didn't believe. I said so and rebelled — so I'd go to hell!

Then they tried to blackmail me. 'If your parents in heaven see you, what will they think?'

'Are you sure they're in heaven?'

'Of course we're sure!'

'Where is it?'

'In the sky.'

'And how do people get up there?'

'By praying, by believing in the true faith and by being obedient.'

'What is faith?'

I asked too many questions. So I, the little she-wolf, recited whatever prayers they wanted and obeyed. I began learning human facial expressions. I learned hypocrisy with ease. The history teacher told me, *'He who knows how to obey knows how to command.'* I wanted to command, so I obeyed.

I became the class prefect and my studies acquired new importance. I devoured books. I had to learn how to express myself without using my fists. I had to cope with an unbearably narrow world which I didn't know and which had been forced on me. I lamented my past suffering in the evenings, and my true nature quickly reasserted itself, as they remarked in despair at each misdemeanour.

'You jumped out of the window again to relieve yourself in the garden!'

'But I've done it before!'

'You were a savage before! A lost soul. Almost an animal.'

'There's nothing wrong with animals!'

'Man is superior. You simply can't behave like that!'

Superior man really got on my nerves and I'd seethe with rage in my room in the evenings, my chin resting on my knees, on a bed that was far too soft, with a crucifix above my head, which frightened me. That man nailed to a cross was awful: just another instance of human beings taking delight in inflicting pain.

Grandpère didn't come and see me. They openly despised his anticlericalism and, as I had a legitimate guardian, he didn't feel he had any right to interfere. He also thought, and he was probably right — that I needed to become a respectable, independent young woman, and that there'd be time for me to live life as I wanted when I was earning a living. In the meantime, I was being well fed, I had somewhere to live and I was receiving an education. I was to sit a competitive examination so that I could be a teacher or, at any rate, look after children.

I had no idea that there were Jewish organisations that could have taken me in, provided information about my parents and maybe helped me recall old memories. It wasn't too late in the day, despite the traumas. But no one even mentioned that they existed in front of me; no one gave me any hope. The good people who took in stray children often brought them up in line with their own religious criteria. Many of them assured these children's salvation during the war.

They were also determined not to think about the war any more. They wanted to rebuild, forget, avoid ferreting through other people's pasts in case they discovered facts that didn't tally with everyone else's experience: the denunciations, the raids, the contempt, the betrayals and the hatred of anything different.

I, on the other hand, was desperate not to obliterate every trace and memory of my experiences. The anger and suffering I endured after the war as a result of not being understood were harder to bear than my lengthy personal war itself, because no one wanted to know about it.

I tried to pay them back, for wanting to turn me into a Catholic and for not taking an interest in my life, by refusing to go to college. 'I'm ill.'

'You're never ill.'

The teachers certainly knew a thing or two, but they'd never come across strength like mine. I was capable of whirling round ready to hit someone coming up behind me. No one, not even they, picked a quarrel with me any more. What happened to me before their very eyes made a great impact on them: right under the teachers' noses, I shut my eyes and dropped to the floor like a stone. Paralysed.

I'd done it on purpose. I didn't even flinch when a doctor pricked me with his needle. I didn't move a muscle. My body obeyed my mind. At that time, in the 1950s, no one was talking about the power of mind over matter. I had the ability, the unhuman determination, to ignore physical pain in my legs and feet; I'd experimented with it on my own throughout my odyssey. When the pain became too much, I knew how to master it. The same was true for hunger, cold and thirst. My strong will immobilised my legs that day. I suppose I did exactly the same when I took the German murderer unawares before springing at him with my knife. Fear and hatred must have prompted that behaviour. This time it was the urge to escape from too much pressure and humiliation.

I shut my eyes while the doctor's needle stimulated my muscles. I ordered them not to twitch and they obeyed. Later on in life, my resistance to pain had its downside because it caused me to neglect some serious health problems.

The immediate outcome was a period of bed-rest. No morning mass, no college

— and the two spinsters fluttering around me like birds had no idea what to do with me. They gave me a notebook so that I could write down anything I wanted. 'Since you can write very well now, why not make the most of it to produce an essay?'

Their brother the priest was supposed to keep me company in the afternoons, so that I wasn't on my own too much while they were teaching at school. It took me some time before I turned to the first page of that little diary and wrote down, in short sentences, everything I'd been through. I filled pages and pages with it . . .

'*I left by crossing the bridge . . . The wolves fed me . . . Marek died, he told me not to forget . . . I looked for my parents in Warsaw . . . Misha gave me a knife . . .*'

I peppered that still-laboured account with small details about my life since I'd been incarcerated in that house. My thoughts on music, which Léontine wanted to teach me, and on geography, which I knew about and for good reason, and which was completely different from the subject taught in school. I included one anecdote, which I didn't consider particularly interesting and which caused me to lose my first essay:

Their brother the priest says I have good teeth and pretty lips. He strokes my shoulders. He says my bust is full and that he likes that very much!'

That notebook was my life story — the long distance I'd travelled before I'd come to their house, then college, the priest who liked to sit close to me. It was probably only about fifteen pages long. It summarised the main points clumsily, but I thought it might prompt them to ask questions, which I could choose to answer or not, or even that they'd simply say, 'So you really did go off looking for your parents, did you?'

I also thought that they'd see me as more than a badly brought-up kid, a piece of human wreckage picked up in the street who had to be straightened out in every way. I was hoping for a positive reaction, in any case. Not yelling. Not to be showered by a deluge of insults!

'How dare you? This is a web of lies! A dog's dinner! You should be ashamed of yourself!'

'This is a wicked fabrication! Do you realise, Léontine, that this girl's soul is blacker than hell!'

Léontine and Sybil ripped up the notebook in self-righteous indignation and burned my wolves, Marek and Misha in the stove they had lit for that purpose. They were mainly concerned with burning the priest's petty indiscretions but, in their spinsterish hysteria, they were also burning my life, my childhood and my suffering, when all I'd been doing was trying to set down that heavy burden.

I'd made no mention in that clumsy essay of a young girl's screams and the blood of a German soldier on my knife. I was too scared of being thought a criminal and thrown into prison. My nightmares were already my prison. In their eyes, though, my life was 'a dog's dinner'. They were fond of that phrase and used it often in connection with me.

I don't know whether they believed that their brother had interfered with me — people didn't talk about 'those things' then — but he stopped coming to their house very often. That poor priest, with his vague repressed desires, hadn't done me any great harm, though. He'd even made me laugh, poor man! Pretty lips? I knew they weren't, and there wasn't a man alive who could catch me out with such a blatant lie. I felt as if everyone was staring at me because I was so ugly. I didn't show it, but I was afraid of other people. I couldn't 'smell' them in the same way as I smelled animals. I thought they were ridiculous, crybabies whining at the merest scratch. When I became a woman, for example, I didn't think anything much of it and didn't say anything to the old maids. So what if I was bleeding? I'd shed so much blood in the past! Sybil noticed and wanted to tell me discreetly about what it meant to be a woman. She wanted to calm me down, and asked if I was in any pain — what a fuss for a little blood! And how needlessly spiteful, how hypocritical, to destroy the little notebook that contained my memories.

I decided to start walking again after a couple of weeks. I didn't trust the spinsters any more. I just wanted to run away, to escape, but unfortunately the only way I could escape was by sitting that wretched teaching exam, and to do that I had to cram three more years of study into a single year.

I was so uncontrollable, so difficult, that they sent me to board in a convent, although I still had a priest as my guardian. I was incarcerated in that convent surrounded by high walls. I had a room on the top floor reserved for students. Lessons were free, but I paid for my board and lodging by working for the sisters. Old people lived on the first and second floors. It was a cheap old people's home with corridors that stank of urine. I wore second-hand rags that had been 'donated'. My wardrobe wasn't at all what I would've liked — I loved bright colours and wanted to live life to the full at any price.

I had one free hour a week, which proved to be some compensation for my mandatory Sunday visit to the spinsters. I had to learn to walk through the streets on my own. The first time I felt both happy and panicky. First I visited all the public gardens in the town, guided by a hazy memory of my father holding my hand in one of those parks. I didn't know which one it was. Then I attempted window-shopping with the other girls so that I could get used to crowds, which still frightened me.

I eventually learned a new type of solitude, the type experienced in towns where I felt heartbreakingly lonely surrounded by others. I found that way of life much harder to bear than the forest, wind, snow, cold or heat. And human beings were so ugly. I felt if I had some animals for company in that human hell, I would be better equipped to deal with the cultural shock. So I adopted a rat. He entered my bedroom through the heating duct which ran upwards through the ceiling of each room in the convent. When I first noticed him, I widened the hole in the floor, and next to it I put down some cheese stolen from the canteen for my new companion.

He soon became a fat, handsome, well-fed

rat and I had to make the hole even wider for him to be able to squeeze through. I'd talk to him just as I used to talk to the free world of the forest, and that relaxed me in the evenings. When I was in bed, he'd sit on his haunches on the blanket, smoothing his whiskers. With my index finger, I'd tickle his stomach and he'd utter little squeaks, which I translated as 'I like being here with you.'

He was the only thing that made me feel better, my only source of comfort. I'd rush to my room when I came out of class, throw my books on to the table, kneel down near the duct and call him: 'Moshe? Moshe? Come and get your cheese, my little prince!'

I'd hear scratching, then his handsome head would pop up, and I'd watch him in delight as he gnawed.

After a while I suspected that Sister Marie, with her plump, red little face, had poisoned Moshe. I threw a tray at her head, screaming that I didn't want to be a Catholic! He had been my only consolation for living in the world of human beings. Later in life, I had all sorts of companions. Dogs and cats as well as a snake, skunks, opossums, does, badgers and birds. I couldn't live without them.

One day, when there was no college, instead of going to visit the spinsters I told them that I had lessons. I went off in search of my childhood, my vanished parents. I didn't want them to be in heaven, as I was continually being told they were. I didn't want the 'angel' who was supposed to be protecting me in their stead. I wanted my mother — her hair, her perfume. I wanted my father who called me his 'beauty'. I looked for the school, the streets, a house with a balcony, and all I brought back were two photographs of strangers who had probably also disappeared in the raids of that hellish period. They have served as my memory. I often contemplate them as I walk past their frame. An unknown woman and an unknown man, my personal memorial which I decorate with flowers every day. Although others may have forgotten them or may have died with them, I have survived to honour them.

Epilogue
Far-off America

I paid a visit to the Town Hall to correct my identity. My name was Mishke, and since arriving at the spinsters' house I hadn't answered to the name of Monique. They'd opted for Monikou, which wasn't any better. I said to the official, 'Good day. The thing is, Monique Valle isn't my real name. I'd like to be registered under my parents' name!'

'I see. And what are they called?'

'Gerusha and Reuven.'

'Yes, but what is their surname?'

'I don't know.'

'But you do have a surname?'

'Yes, but it's not mine.'

'Listen! You already have a surname registered here. What more do you want?'

'But it isn't mine!'

'There's nothing we can do about that, *ma petite*. Don't make life difficult for yourself.

You already have a surname, so why not hold on to it!'

I went back there on another occasion. They must have thought I was mad. I told myself that surnames weren't really important and made an identity card for myself. Mishke, daughter of Gerusha and Reuven, born 12 May 1934. I'd decided to keep 12 May, since I imagined that the people forging my new papers had at least left that unchanged. And that the M for Monique was there as a reminder of Mishke. As for Valle, I regarded it as Grandpère's surname more than anything, so I put up with it.

I passed my exam, which I'd retaken after narrowly failing it once, but I couldn't see myself being a teacher for the rest of my life. What I taught children wasn't found in schoolbooks. I took them for walks, I told them stories about animals and I explained the world to them in my own way. They loved my approach, but it didn't appeal to adults. I couldn't bear my life being dictated by that convent any more.

I went to see Grandpère, who'd been forbidden to visit the convent. He was growing old on his own in a small apartment, but freedom was still just as sacred to him: 'Live your life. Hang up your second-hand clothes. You can always bed down here.'

I only had to stay there for a week. Luck smiled on me for the first time: I found a job with a shipping company. I promised Grandpère that as soon as I was 'rich', we would live together. By now I was well past the age of eighteen, and I went looking for adventure in order to escape a narrow society bounded by principles I didn't believe in. I chose the world.

I boarded a boat travelling between Belgium and the Congo. I was a stewardess, and my job was to look after any children on board for the voyage. I was earning my living and had broken free from the suffocating protection of the convent. I had a good wage, my own place and — even though I knew nothing about all the paraphernalia involved in living life as a free woman, such as rental contracts, invoices and electricity bills — I managed.

Those boats were transporting spices and fruit, as well as occasional passengers, either on their way back to Belgium or heading out to the Congo. It was a miniature world, a timeless floating town. I wore an attractive uniform with gold braid, and a cap — new clothes, just for me. I wanted my new-found freedom to sparkle. I wanted to forget the unhappiness that clung to me like a second skin and even the memory of that unhappiness. I took huge bites of life. I was life personified. This was an explosive period. I wanted everything. I wanted to have a good time, meet men, drink, have fun, dance — and I did all those things to excess. I was enjoying life like a sailor, living it up in every port.

That big iron boat smelling of spices took me to the port of Matadi, in the former Belgian Congo, at the mouth of the river now known as the Zaire. This was in the heart of Africa, a country that smelled strongly of wild animals, and I loved it.

There was no one on the quay waiting to take me anywhere and no one waiting for me to come back, so between each port of call I continued to do what I always did: I talked to myself, to the clouds and to the animals. But I was now writing. I took my black notebooks everywhere with me; I even scrawled on beermats. And as soon as I could, I'd dash off to a bar, the Guest House, in Matadi, to let my hair down with the sailors.

The captain often said kindly to me, 'Don't forget you're a girl!' He'd pull out his hair in despair when I went off drinking and rampaging with the crew. On those evenings stools would fly through the air, the pilots stationed in Kamina would be thrashed by our sailors or vice versa, and we'd come back on board to dress our wounds and tend our bruises. 'I can't forbid you to go ashore,' said my gallant captain, 'but, the devil take it, you're a woman!'

I'd drink anything — rum, beer, brandy, whisky — and some mornings I'd wake up in my cabin with my head at the bottom of the bed and no idea how I'd got there. But I was no longer drunk on tragedy. I didn't want to demoralise or forgive anyone, and when I slipped into an eye-catching dress to go out, I'd think, 'I'm dressed to kill tonight!' Killing meant seducing men, twisting them round my little finger, then casting them away like a used handkerchief. That was my own private depression.

When I came back to Belgium to see Grandpère, I didn't even attempt to ask him whether I looked like my mother. Every time I began a sentence, he'd raise his hand as if to ward off a blow: 'Forget about it. Move on. Don't look back.'

I don't know if he knew something about my parents, but I don't think so. In the last year of his life, we lived together as I'd promised. I was looking around for a little apartment to buy and he said, 'I'll make up the shortfall,' which is what he did. I was able to buy a small apartment — the size of a pocket handkerchief. I had the impression

310

that he was using the money he'd saved from his pension to reimburse me for the envelope of cash that had been handed over by the woman in black in exchange for my protection.

He really became my Grandpère. He never said it, but he loved me more than anyone, and after he had died in his bed one sad winter evening, I did as he'd asked: 'I don't want anyone to come to my funeral.' I went to the cemetery only once to keep him company; I never went back. I hate cemeteries. My parents have no grave. I preferred to put flowers near his portrait by 'his' armchair rather than mourn for him in a place that stirred up many fearful memories for me. I wanted him still alive, with his shrewd smile under his large moustache. I can still hear him saying, 'Jump! Don't be afraid of being afraid!'

In Matadi, the blacks from the villages poured into the white town, causing such an eruption of panic that the whites fled, even though they weren't able to escape the massacre. Luck no longer smiled on me. Every voyage back to Belgium repatriated more dead men lying in the hold. Another war. Renewed dread prompted by the hatred in the eyes of black sailors.

The wind of adventure had shifted and,

311

one morning, after one last night of alcohol-fuelled craziness, I looked at myself in the mirror and said, 'That's enough. You won't find oblivion in a glass of whisky or in men's desire. 'We' shall make a fresh start, 'we' are going to change direction.' That was the last drop of alcohol ever to pass my lips.

Congolese independence meant that I had to give up my job and begin looking for another. I wanted to marry, have a family. I made a mistake about the man, the love and the family. He was a Sephardic Jew and he entered a loveless marriage with me to take advantage of my apartment. My only family was the son he left me — without too many regrets; I never saw him again.

I used my experience of life to bring up my son. I wouldn't let anyone else hold him when he was a baby. I wanted him to carry my smell, not that of another human being. I taught him not to be afraid of being on his own when I was out working for us both. I told him that the world could be explored on foot, on horseback or by car, and that a mother protected her child until he decided to leave. When he grew up, that's what my son did. He's just as tough as I was, perhaps even tougher, and just as adventurous and intrepid. He lives a long way from me and he has his own pack, just as a young wolf should.

One day, I asked him if he missed having his biological father around. He answered, 'My father is the man who raised me and took care of me.'

I met that man when my son was still a child. Maurice has been my husband and the father of my son for over thirty years. He soothed my nightmares, because I still couldn't talk about my childhood and sometimes I used to cry out during the night. I told him all about my youthful escapades when I was eager to live life to the full, but he guessed that all of that had deeper, invisible roots. 'Talk to me. Tell me what's wrong.'

I trusted him. He was similar to me in that he didn't need anyone but us. He loved animals and looked after me like a father or mother would have done despite being younger than me. He had Grandpère's wisdom and Marthe's caring ways. He solved all my problems. I could finally rest, stop fighting and fall asleep in his arms, cradled like a child.

'Tell me about your nightmare,' he urged me gently. But still I resisted. I found it hard to trust this human love. He thought I was beautiful and he tried to boost my confidence. I'd certainly grown into a beautiful woman by then, but I didn't see myself that way. All I could see were my scars, my deformed feet, my wildness. I'd bitten him more than once by way of arguing a point in our discussions; I still harboured that inner animal fierceness. He wanted me to accept that not all human beings were hateful, but that was too much to ask of me at that time.

I was living through every stage in my life simultaneously: my childhood, my youth and my womanhood. I was genuinely in love, and when he was away I felt awful. I wanted him with me all the time and, in the evening, the comfort of falling asleep next to him, of feeling safe. I became dependent on him without even noticing. I sometimes felt such deep despair when the past claimed me that Maurice was terribly afraid of what he called my highs and lows.

The mere sight of tram number 56 — now the modern, aerodynamic 103 — would send me into a new fit of rage at not knowing what had become of my mother. What they had done to her. At night, I'd wake up dripping with sweat, terrified. 'Her hair! What did they do with her hair?' Paradoxically, though, I still didn't believe she was dead. My parents were alive somewhere, in Russia. She couldn't get out of the country, but one day she would come back. This utopian idea comforted me, while stories about the concentration camps plunged me into a black depression.

314

The nightmares occurred less frequently thanks to Maurice's love, but they still encapsulated the unbearable, searing memory of my childhood, and the slightest clash with society or an individual could trigger a frenzied rage — which Maurice always did his best to control.

We moved house, because some neighbours had carved a Star of David on our door and letterbox. Maurice knew I was capable of reaching for a gun at times like that. We argued about it. 'Just walk away. You place too much importance on stupid acts like this,' he said. Maurice is too accepting of human beings. He is tolerant and kind. He doesn't suffer fools gladly, but he also doesn't let them get to him.

I was hypersensitive and found it impossible not to fight violence with violence. I was still afraid that the Nazi horror would be repeated. Human nature had been capable of producing it, so I felt I had to turn my back on humanity for ever. We went to live in Holland, where Maurice had an excellent job. I chose our house because our little dog Jimmy had cocked his leg against that particular gate and not another! I was still an injured child, clinging to signs from my animal family like a lifeline. My human skin didn't fit properly. I loved Jimmy, although he was a real terror who'd occasionally bite us. He was my little wolf and sometimes he would howl like a wolf, with his ears laid back and his muzzle in the air, which always filled me with delight.

Holland smelled like happiness for five years. My son was living with us; I had a garden, my animals, space. We took long bike trips and travelled widely — to Sweden, Italy, France, Spain, Israel and Arizona, because I loved the desert and the heat, the snakes and the scorpions, the desert flowers which bloom for just one night and then die at daybreak.

I was still walking badly, and Maurice decided that I should have an operation. I should have felt liberated when my feet, which had carried so much suffering and so many memories, were restored to normal, but I still didn't talk. My nightmares had lessened during those years of near happiness, but I still wanted to run. To go further away, leave Europe and walk on fresh soil without any memories. I wanted America.

In America, gradually I began to open up. Maurice listened and comforted me. He also saw me begin writing again. He was patient, encouraging and discreet. He allowed me to unpack my bag, set down suitcases that had been too heavy for me to carry for so many years. He now knew about the horrors that woke me at night shaking with fear. The only thing I still didn't dare tell him about was the knife I'd plunged into that German soldier's stomach. I'd killed. I couldn't confess, as if I were really a criminal and would be sentenced for it.

I still refused to see a psychiatrist. Maurice had managed to persuade me several times to try, but I'd always come back discouraged by the mediocrity of the remarks they made. Did they think I was mad just because I didn't like human beings? It was easier for them to assume that than to make the effort to understand me.

I then made proper contact with a Jewish community for the first time. I'd already tried in Europe, and the rabbi I'd seen had asked me straight out, 'Are you sure you're Jewish?' I'd walked out, slamming the door behind me. I always came up against that wall, that gulf, the impossibility of being accepted just on the strength of my parents' first names and my memories of a shattered childhood. The American rabbi simply listened to what I had to say and accepted it. I studied Hebrew and remembered my mother's prayers. I could talk about her in peace.

But Jimmy died. My dog, my wolf, passed away, the last link I had with my memories of Belgium. I can't explain why that death triggered everything. I was out of my mind with grief, obsessed by the death of that animal, as if I had just lost my parents all over again. It was much more than a bereavement. I'd already been upset by the death of another animal, a cat, whose last moments had been spent far away from me at the vet's. I couldn't bear the idea of a creature I loved dying so far away. If it dies in your arms, that's different, you're with it until it draws its last breath, you've comforted it to the end. Jimmy's death somehow encapsulated all the deaths I'd experienced — my mother's, my father's, Grandpère's, Marthe's — as well as all those I'd seen, all the corpses throughout my childhood. I began to have even more nightmares. The bloody knife, the children being gunned down, Marek . . . I screamed through the night. I scratched at my old wounds until they bled, like before. I completed my own course of therapy after that bereavement by making a short film about my dog so that a part of him remained, so that he wouldn't be forgotten. Deep down, I didn't want to forget anything. It seemed to me that the worst thing anyone could do was to forget. I'd been forced to do that too often. Forget the past, forget the war, forget you're Jewish. Forget the wolves and your dog; you'll have another. No.

Like a heartbroken kid, I put together a sequence of images recreating the absolute love I felt for Jimmy, as if I wanted the whole world to see my grief. To accept my love of animals at long last.

One day, I discovered a regional park where a wonderful, eccentric man, motivated by a deep love of wolves, had decided to protect them and teach people about them. Although that man is now dead, his wife continues his life work. Through him, I was able to renew my contact with wolves, with their smell, their fur, their leaps, their fights, their games. The pleasure it gave me was indescribable. I brought them fresh meat; I delighted in watching them devour it, hearing them howl and being able to howl with them from time to time.

It was quite by chance that everything was set in motion. My rabbi at that time, Yocheved Helligman, asked me to tell my story on the day of Yom HaShoa, Holocaust Remembrance Day. Did I speak! Hell, how I spoke and wept! Then I was invited to speak at other temples, in universities such as Brandeis, Smith, Amherst, New York and others. For the first time, I spoke about that German soldier who'd raped, killed and spat on a very young girl, and who would've killed me too without a moment's thought. But this had been war, it had been him or me, and I'd had the will to survive at any price. Remember that an animal will defend itself against death with ten times the strength of any human, and I was that animal.

At one lecture, a woman said to me, 'You're not a holocaust survivor. You didn't live in the camps.' Hers was just one voice among others. It shouldn't have upset me as it did, but I was annoyed with myself for telling the world a story that wasn't universally accepted, just because it wasn't like everyone else's. I was different, as always — not really Jewish, not really a survivor. Naturally, most of my audiences stood by me, helped me regain a foothold in life. Naturally, some of the remarks I found hurtful might have been tactless but they weren't meant to be malicious. Naturally, I could count on my friends, who know that loving isn't about invading someone's privacy but about giving them room to breathe, and who respect my boundaries.

Nevertheless, I withdrew into my shell. I didn't want to talk any more. I'd thought I'd find it liberating and I'd been wrong. One particularly difficult day, Maurice said to me, 'You really must talk to a psychiatrist.'

I didn't want to. I went under duress, just to please Maurice, and, miracle of miracles, a woman managed to loosen that invisible knot of suffering. She'd read my story, which helped because I didn't have to tell her about it all over again. I could tell her about my attempts to live my life after I'd survived. I began a proper course of therapy with her. I realised that, for example, the death of my she-wolf was the death of my mother; that when my dog Jimmy died, this was also my mother's death. That I hadn't been allowed to mourn during my childhood and that it was quite natural that, as an adult, I should still be searching for her and always would be, even in the heart of a wolf.

She realised that I was still trapped in my childhood. I still amassed provisions — blankets and shoes in particular! Everything I'd needed on my travels through Germany, Poland and the Ukraine. I stockpiled them in case of a war which wasn't likely to happen but which I still feared. I filled my house with cuddly toys. I rushed off to buy a hobby horse just like Jules. I surrounded myself with objects to fill an immense emptiness, so vast that it still made me giddy. I locked myself away when I craved space. Fear would make me reel in the midst of crowds. I hated the town because I'd fled it for too long fearing that I'd be caught. I changed my name the way some people change their shoes. When I was walking, I'd called myself Mishke; now I rushed around adopting any name that appealed to me in Europe. I was searching for an identity that would help me forget, without ever finding it. Until, one day, I chose Misha, in memory of the kind man I'd met in the Ukraine, then Myriam for the rabbi, because Mishke is a Yiddish form of Myriam.

I gave myself permission to love what I wanted to love. My husband, my son, my animals, my solitude, far from human beings whom I still found threatening. In America, I'd found the space I needed for another type of survival: my need to survive the memories.

Nothing is perfect. Survival wasn't easy. We lost our house, my sanctuary, Maurice lost his job, we lived by our wits, doing without in order to feed the cats and dogs, birds, coyotes and wolves in the vicinity. I shook with fear again one September 11th on soil that I'd believed was safe from war. Did I have to begin running again?

I didn't run. I started writing again and saying freely what I still needed to say, so that I could be free, once and for all. But I've forgotten nothing. My memory belongs to my parents. They will never grow old, will never die, because I think about them every day.

Today, I dream of owning a patch of land far from the noise and violence of human life, where I will recreate my earthly paradise in peace and quiet among tall trees, my beloved firs and silver birches, and fill it with animals and birdsong. There I shall build a comfortable house where I'll make my nest and there I shall erect a memorial dedicated to those whom I didn't see die, but whom I've mourned so deeply.

Gerusha my mother, Reuven my father, those unknown victims of the holocaust.

Zog nit keynmol az du geyst dem letztn veg
Never say that you are walking your final road

Acknowledgements

Friends have come, friends have gone, some have betrayed me and others welcomed me in for a time when I was homeless. I'd like to thank those who, in the face of all opposition, have remained my friends throughout the most difficult of times and also those who by becoming my friends have widened the circle.

In particular, I'd like to thank Ramona Hamblin, my lawyer, who ensured the triumph of truth and justice and who never abandoned me and later also Stephen Sheehy; the McCaffrey family, the start of my new life in America; Odette Sullivan, the fighter; Meredith and Jon Kilgore, forces of nature; Helen Rice; Judy and Ron Lane; Natalie and Peter Bosse; Bert and Lilly Arling; Rabbi Al Friedman and his wife, Audrey; Rabbi Yocheved Helligman; *my pal* Janet Nirenberg, still at my side; the

Bloomstein family; Sandy Jimbetty; Diane Marrazzo; Pat Cunningham; the McCarron family; Paul and Rose, from the Enchanted Fox; Naomi Eigner Price; Wayne and Adrienne Domeier; Arlene and Frank Ruisi; Nina and Lee Spedoni, who knew the liberation of Paris — Lee having fought in Normandy; Donna Trifan, ever loyal; Joni Soffron, of the wolves; Rina and Steve Gaffin; Jeffrey and Sue Steele, veterinarians; Jeffrey DiPaola and Suzanne Starr and Dr Medcraft, my current veterinarians; Sandy, Nancy, Debby, Shawn, Jo Beth and Joseph, their staff.

And the extended American circle: Melissa Shepard, the tough one; Anna Mae Grout, the funny one; Rich Lapierre, who suffered a terrible loss and understands; Roberta O'Connell, who found me a little place where I can live in peace; and, of course, all my Canadian friends.

And across the ocean: Arlette Huygh, whom I've known for forty years; my buddy Luc Herman; Margot and Daniel; Janine Houtekier, a loyal, generous friend; Andrea and Stefaan Dumery, a patch of Flemish soil; Liliane and Freddy Lehman and Simone and Harry Bronitz; Eric Monami the loyal; the Botter family in Holland, for years of happiness; Eric Krauthammer in Switzerland.

I would like those who are too numerous to be mentioned here to know that I have not forgotten them. They are of all races and creeds, they are citizens of the world, they are my brothers and sisters in friendship. They know who they are.

I'm deeply grateful to all those people throughout the world who stand against unwarranted spitefulness and cruelty and who strive to protect nature and the animal kingdom.

And, of course, this is not to forget my patient husband, Maurice, my strength, my protective shield; my son, Morris Levy, of whom I am so proud and who loves the far north, and his wife Louise; and obviously all my other 'children', whether of fur, feathers, hair or scales, who encircle me with love; they are my world, my *amours d'amour*.

I'm grateful to Monsieur Bernard Fixot from Editions XO, my French publisher, and his team of enthusiastic young women for their support and encouragement during the long, difficult process of baring my wounds to the world; and, last but not least, I'd like to thank my very dear Marie-Thérèse Cuny, my sister in adversity: her sensitivity and her remarkable ability to understand others have enabled her to express the violent emotions of hatred, rage, fear, life and death as well as my love of wolves with wonderful immediacy, just as I experienced them in all their original intensity; thank you, Marie, without you none of this would have been possible.

We do hope that you have enjoyed reading this large print book.

Did you know that all of our titles are available for purchase?

We publish a wide range of high quality large print books including:
Romances, Mysteries, Classics
General Fiction
Non Fiction and Westerns

Special interest titles available in large print are:
The Little Oxford Dictionary
Music Book
Song Book
Hymn Book
Service Book

Also available from us courtesy of Oxford University Press:
Young Readers' Dictionary
(large print edition)
Young Readers' Thesaurus
(large print edition)

For further information or a free brochure, please contact us at:
Ulverscroft Large Print Books Ltd.,
The Green, Bradgate Road, Anstey,
Leicester, LE7 7FU, England.
Tel: (00 44) 0116 236 4325
Fax: (00 44) 0116 234 0205

Other titles published by
The House of Ulverscroft:

STATUES WITHOUT SHADOWS

Anna Swan

Anna's parents should never have met. He was the son of down-at-heel aristocrats; she was the child of a mining family. In 1950s London, they inhabited an idealistic but brittle world of writers and journalists. Anna was born in 1960, as their marriage was falling apart. By the age of seven, both her parents were dead. Brought up by her grandparents, believing her mother had died of cancer and her father of pneumonia, it wasn't until her late twenties that Anna uncovered the disturbing truth about her parents' glittering and early lives.

MOVING MOUNTAINS

Claire Bertschinger

In Ethiopia in 1984, Claire Bertschinger, an International Red Cross nurse, was filmed surrounded by thousands of starving people and with limited supplies. She had the terrible task of choosing which children to feed, knowing that those she turned away might not last the night. Those shocking pictures inspired Bob Geldof: and, ultimatately, Live Aid . . . Twenty years later Michael Buerk, whose television reports first showed those pictures, persuaded Claire to return to Ethiopia. Claire had always been haunted by the memory of having to make such terrible choices, but the survivors, calling her 'Mamma Claire', welcomed her back with open arms.

JUST A BOY

Richard McCann

Richard McCann was just five when his mother became the first victim of Peter Sutcliffe, the man who came to be known as the 'Yorkshire Ripper'. He and his three sisters, forced to return to their estranged father, were never allowed to heal or forget, their grief caught up in the media circus of a serial killer. Yet Richard and his eldest sister Sonia were forced to endure violent abuse and keep the silence of forgotten children. This is the moving and inspirational story of how two small children stuck together through unimaginable pain and just when they hit rock-bottom, on the road to ruining their own lives forever, decided to make a change.

TWO STEPS BACKWARD

Susie Kelly

Susie Kelly and her husband Terry dreamed of a home in France. With their dogs, parrots and horses, they moved to a farmhouse in the Poitou-Charentes region. While Terry worked in England, Susie had to contend with a homicidal gas cooker, burst pipes and a biting guinea fowl. The enormity of what they had taken on seemed overwhelming, and when Terry came close to death, the dream threatened to turn into a nightmare. But the kindness of the local community inspired them to make a new life for themselves in the place they now call home.

THE TERMINAL MAN

Sir Alfred Mehran and Andre Donkin

Mehran Karimi Nasseri, better known as 'Sir Alfred', has been living in the departure lounge of Terminal 1 of Charles de Gaulle Airport, Paris, for sixteen years. He sleeps on a bench, dines at McDonalds, and is surrounded by piles of magazines and his extensive diary. He arrived at the airport on 8th August 1988, intending to take a plane to London. Without the proper documentation he quickly found himself trapped in a bureaucratic catch-22 nightmare. Fearing arrest as an illegal immigrant if he left the terminal building, he has been waiting while lawyers and government officials argued about his case. This is his incredible story in his own words.

Misha's travels 1941 - 1945